Paradigm

Fifth Edition

KEYBOARDING

Sessions 1–30

All New Web-based Software!

William Mitchell
Ronald Kapper

Editor Tom Modl
Cover and Text Designer Leslie Anderson
Desktop Publisher Lisa Beller

Reviewers/Consultants, 5e:

Sherrie Burke
Hillsborough Community College
Tampa, Florida

Helen Hustead
Westmoreland County Community College
Youngwood, Pennsylvania

Reviewers/Consultants, 4e:

Nancy LaTour
Corning Community College
Corning, New York

Linda Mallinson
Orlando Technical College
Orlando, Florida

Sherrie Burke
Hillsborough Community College
Tampa, Florida

Sherry Foster
Davenport College
Granger, Indiana

Publishing Management Team
Bob Cassel, Publisher; Jeanne Allison, Senior Acquisitions Editor; Janice Johnson, Vice President of Marketing; Shelley Clubb, Electronic Design and Production Manager

ISBN 0-7638-2311-2 (textbook)
ISBN 0-7638-2310-4 (textbook and user guide), Order Number 01613

Published by EMC Corporation
875 Montreal Way
St. Paul, MN 55102
(800) 535-6865
E-mail: educate@emcp.com
Web site: www.emcp.com

Printed in the United States of America
10 9 8 7 6 5 4 3 2 1

Table of Contents

Introduction

Paradigm Keyboarding: Sessions 1–30, Fifth Edition provides instruction in developing the basic keyboarding skills needed to key alphabetic, numeric, and special symbol characters, as well as teaching the skills needed to use a 10-key numeric keypad.

Learning Outcomes

When you have completed this book, you will be able to demonstrate a basic-level mastery of keyboarding, which includes:

- Keying straight-copy alphanumeric material at an average rate of 25 words a minute (WAM) with two or fewer errors per minute
- Keying numeric copy using correct touch techniques on the 10-key numeric keypad at 25 WAM
- Using keyboarding skills to compose coherent material with correct word usage at the word, sentence, paragraph, and document levels

Program Overview

This textbook works in conjunction with Paradigm's Web-based keyboarding and word processing software, Paradigm Keyboarding with Snap (PKB). This software provides you with drill lines and timings for learning keys along with activities for learning language and composition skills.

Session Structure

Sessions 1–30 follow a basic pattern of On-Screen and Textbook exercises.

On-Screen Exercises

- **Warm-Up:** As the name implies, this introductory exercise has you flexing your fingers and practicing key presses so you are ready to key quickly and efficiently when the new material is presented.
- **New Keys:** The computer keyboard is shown on the screen with the new keys highlighted along with instructions for which fingers to use on the new keys.

- **New Key Drills:** The Paradigm software presents a line at a time of words or sentences using the new keys. You are asked to key the lines so your brain and fingers learn where the keys are, and you don't have to look at the keyboard—eventually!
- **Thinking Drills:** These drills are designed to reinforce the English language skills, especially for English Language Learners. They teach you to compose sentences at the keyboard, and to think and key at the same time, eliminating the need to write down what you want to say on paper first. These drills begin in Session 3 and appear in most of the Sessions from 3 to 23.

Textbook Exercises

- **Reinforcement:** In this part of the session, you will key drills similar to those presented on the screen earlier, along with some new ones, in order to reinforce the learning you did on screen.
- **Timings:** This final session activity is an opportunity for you to determine your keyboarding speed and accuracy. The PKB software displays information about the length of the timing and the paragraph and page number in the text. The program's automatic timer begins when you strike the first key. When the time is up, the keyboard locks so you cannot continue. Immediately the software checks the accuracy and length of what you keyed and displays the results in WAM and errors at the bottom of the screen. The software also automatically saves this file to your directory, and you can print it when required. In addition, the software keeps a record of your timing scores. This record is called the "Timing Performance Report," and can be accessed from your Paradigm Keyboarding with Snap home page.
- **Ergonomic Tips:** An awareness and informational tip pertaining to ergonomics will appear at the end of each session.

Ergonomically Preparing Your Work Environment

A comfortable and ergonomic work environment is essential to efficient keyboarding. Your workstation needs to contain only those items necessary for working on the sessions. Here is an ergonomic checklist to review before you begin:

- Align the front of the keyboard with the desk's front edge.
- Adjust the monitor so your line of sight is 10–20 degrees below the horizontal.
- Adjust your chair so that you sit about 16 to 24 inches from the screen and your chair seat is 16–19 inches from the floor.
- Sit up straight, back against the chair, feet flat on the floor.
- Place your fingers on the keys in a curved position. Raise your forearms and wrists slightly so that they are parallel to the keyboard. Do not rest your forearms on the keyboard!

Hardware and Software Required to Use PKB

To use the PKB software, you will need the following equipment and configuration:

Processor	Intel Celeron 600Mhz or higher.
Operating System	Windows 2000 (with SP4) or Windows XP Home/Professional (with SP1 or Higher)
RAM	128 MB minimum (256 MB highly recommended on Windows XP)
Web Browser	Internet Explorer 6.0
Desktop Resolution	800 x 600 in 16 bit color

Security Information for Windows and Internet Explorer

1. Scripting and cookies must be enabled within Internet Explorer.
2. Pop-up blocking software must be disabled for www.keyboarding.emcp.com.
3. The web browser should permit signed ActiveX controls to be installed and activated.
4. Computer firewalls should be set to accept data transfer to and from www.keyboarding.emcp.com.
5. Administrative privileges are required to install the ActiveX control for the first time. (Win XP)
6. Power user (or higher) privileges are required to install the ActiveX control for the first time. (Win 2000)
7. Once the Active X control is installed, PKB can be run with the privileges of a guest account.

Preparing Internet Explorer for Viewing and Using PKB

In order to use the PKB software that is part of your textbook package, you need to have access to a computer that is connected to the Internet, has either the Windows 2000 or Windows XP operating system, with the Internet Explorer 6.0 Web browser. You will need to make the following adjustments in Internet Explorer to ensure that you can access and use PKB.

Disabling Pop-Up Blockers

Pop-up blockers need to be turned off in order for you to view PKB. If your computer has Windows XP with Service Pack 2 installed on it, you will need to take the following steps to ensure that PKB's popup windows are functional:

1. Click Tools on Internet Explorer's Menu bar.
2. Point to the Pop-up Blocker and click Pop-up Blocker Settings.
3. In the dialog that appears, type in **keyboarding.emcp.com** and click the Add button.
4. Click the Close button.

Installing the ActiveX Control

Take the following steps to ensure that your Internet Explorer settings permit the ActiveX control needed to use the keyboarding software can be launched:

To ensure that Active X controls and plug-ins are enabled in Internet Explorer, take the following steps:

1. Click Tools and then click Internet Options.
2. Click the Security Tab.
3. Select Internet from the list of zones displayed. The security level for this zone should be set at "Medium." If not, follow any of the methods mentioned below.

Method 1 - Utilizing the Default Zone Security Settings (Recommended)

1 Click the Default Level button.
2 Verify that the security level slider is set to the Medium Security Level.
3 Click the Apply button, and then click OK.

Method 2 - Customizing the Internet Zone Security Settings

1 Click the Custom Level button.
2 Navigate to the section entitled ActiveX controls and plug-ins.
3 Locate the heading entitled Download signed ActiveX controls and click Prompt.
4 Locate the heading entitled Script ActiveX controls marked safe for scripting and click Enable.
5 Navigate to the section entitled Downloads.
6 Locate the heading entitled File download and click Enable.
7 Navigate to the section entitled Scripting.
8 Locate the heading Active scripting and click Enable.
9 Click OK to save your changes.
10 Click OK again to shut the window.

Download signed ActiveX controls
Disable
Enable
Prompt

Script ActiveX controls marked safe for scripting
Disable
Enable
Prompt

File download
Disable
Enable

Active scripting
Disable
Enable
Prompt

Using the Paradigm Keyboarding with Snap Software

Getting Started: Beginning a Session

Below are detailed instructions and illustrations for entering and exiting PKB. These instructions are also given in Session 1 and then repeated in the next two sessions.

1 Log on to the Internet if your computer is not already connected to it.
2 At the Windows desktop of your computer, double-click the *Internet Explorer* icon.
3 At the Internet Explorer screen, click on the entry in the Address text box.
4 Key **www.keyboarding.emcp.com** in the Address text box and click *GO*. The Paradigm Keyboarding with Snap home page appears.

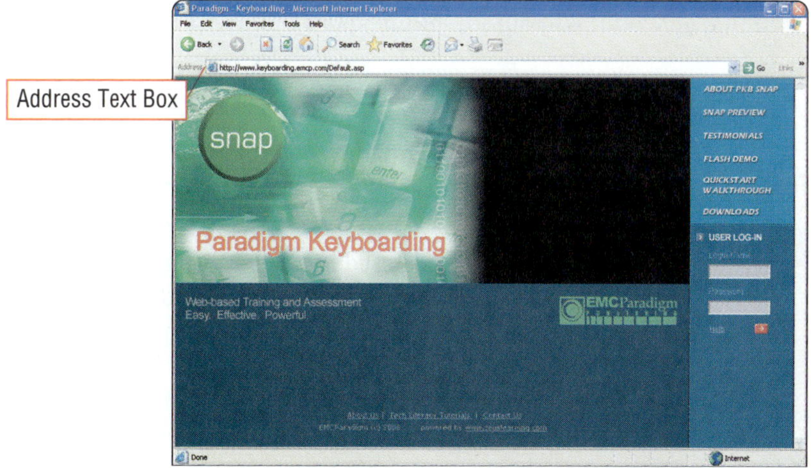

5 Your instructor has given you a **login name** that has been assigned for your class. The textbook package for your course includes a *Paradigm Keyboarding with Snap User Guide*. On the inside front cover of the *User Guide* is your unique PKB **password** that you will use with the login name from your instructor to access PKB. Enter your login name in the Login Name text box (lower right corner of the screen). Enter your password in the Password text box.

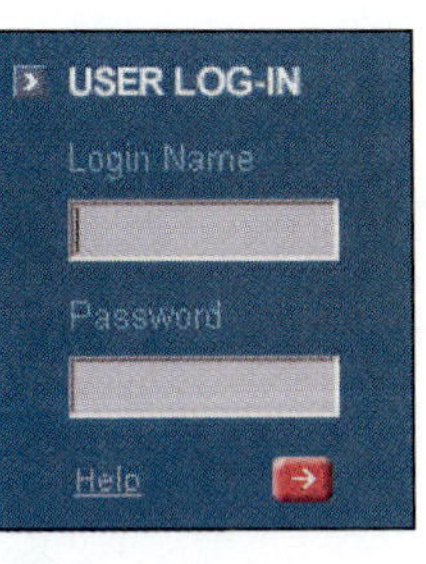

6 Click the arrow in the red box.

Note: *If you enter either your login name or password incorrectly, you will receive an error message, stating that you need to try again. You must re-type your login details exactly; login names and passwords are case sensitive. If you have forgotten your login name or password, please contact your instructor.*

7 When you log into Paradigm Keyboarding for the first time, you will be asked to read and agree to the Paradigm Keyboarding End User License Agreement, and to verify certain details about your course. You will need to do this only once.

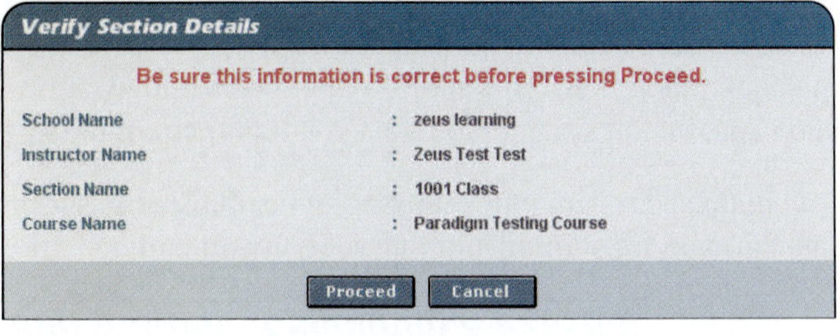

If the information displayed at this point is correct, click the Proceed button to continue.

Note: *If the information displayed does not match your course details, click Cancel and contact your instructor to get the correct Login Name for your section. If you discover you are in the wrong section after you have already enrolled, ask your instructor to have you moved to the correct section.*

8 Your Paradigm Keyboarding with Snap Welcome page appears.

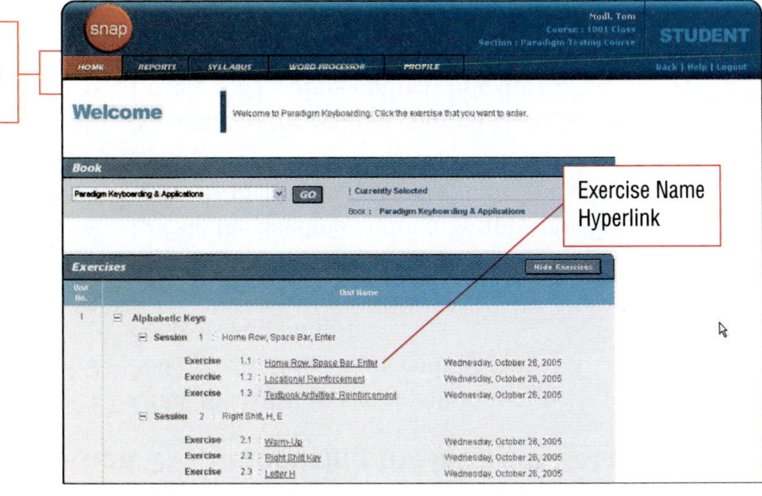

9 Find the session and exercise you want to launch in the Exercises table, and click the exercise name hyperlink once. The Launch Keyboarding dialog box appears.

10 Click the Launch button.

11 The PKB Exercise screen appears.

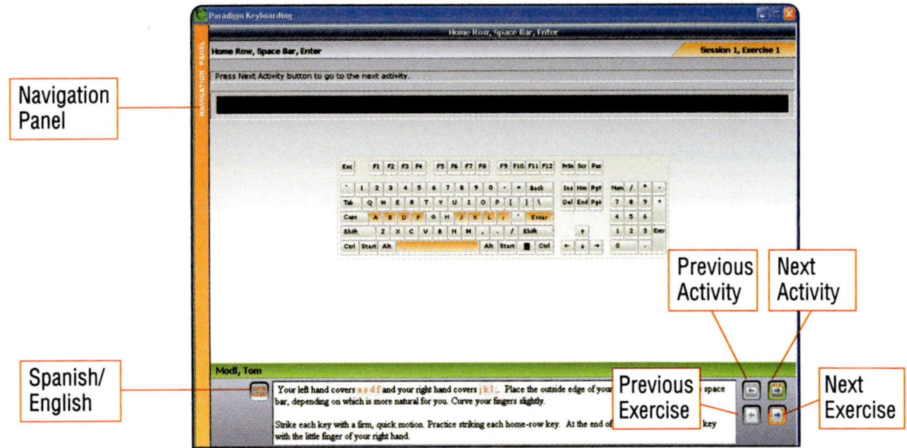

Essential Program Commands and Features

The PKB Exercise screen features the following buttons and functions:

Next Activity/Previous Activity These buttons take you to the next or previous activity within an exercise.

Next Exercise/Previous Exercise These buttons take you to the next or previous exercise of the program. These will provide the most common way of moving through the program.

Navigation Panel This feature allows you to move to any exercise within the program. Click on the orange panel with your mouse and a tree menu showing all the sessions and exercises in the program appears.

Spanish/English This toggle button allows you to view most software instructions in Spanish. Click the button to see instructions in Spanish. Click it again to see them in English.

When exercises are done from the text, two more icons appear at the bottom-left side of the screen. They are—

- A Timing button where you can set a time length for a specified time period. At the end of the timing, the software calculates your Words-a-Minute (WAM) rate, and adds that to your work.
- A WAM button where you have an open ended time frame; when you click on the Stop WAM button which replaced the WAM button, when the document or timing is completed, the software calculates your Words-a-Minute (WAM) rate.

An important point to remember about these buttons is that the button does not work if the program is requiring some other specific response (for example, a dialog box is displayed and the program is waiting for you to respond). However, once the response has been completed, the PKB buttons will function.

Ending a Session

At the end of each session, you have three options: print any documents you have created, continue with the next session, or exit PKB.

Print

To print exercises proceed as follows:

1. Click the Close button in the top right corner of the PKB Exercise screen.
2. At your Paradigm Keyboarding with Snap Welcome page, point to Reports on the Snap menu bar, and click View Submissions Report.
3. At the View Submissions Report Wizard, click Show session files to see drill and reinforcement text, or Show timings files to see the timings text.
4. Click Show Report.
5. Click the name of the file you want to print.
6. At the Word Processor dialog box, click Launch.
7. Click File, and then click Print.
8. At the Print dialog box, click OK.
9. Click the Close button to close the Paradigm Word Processor.
10. Click Home on the Snap menu bar to return to the Welcome page.

Continue

To continue on to the next session, click the Next Exercise button.

Exit

To exit PKB, take the following steps:

1. Click the Close button in the top right corner of the PKB Exercise screen.
2. At your Paradigm Keyboarding with Snap Welcome page, click Logout.

Program Hints

At this point, you are ready to begin working in the program. Here are some hints to help you move smoothly and efficiently through the sessions:

- Be sure the computer you are using has the proper settings for accessing the PKB software. See the section "Using the Paradigm Keyboarding with Snap Software" above or your *Paradigm Keyboarding with Snap User Guide* for details.
- Whenever a dialog box is displayed, you must respond to it before trying to execute another program command.
- All session work is named and saved automatically:
  1. Warm-Ups, New-key drills, Thinking Drills, Timed Short Drills, and Reinforcement exercises are saved in a file called 000ses (where 000 is the session number and "ses" stands for session).
  2. Timings are saved in a file called 000tim (where 000 is the session number and "tim" stands for timing).
- All printing is done using the Paradigm Word Processor (PWP), except in the Reinforcement activities, where you have the option of printing from the screen. You can access the files created by PKB through the View Submissions Report available through the Reports menu of your PKB Home page. (See the instructions above under "Ending a Session" on how to access this report and print files.)

Now you are ready to proceed with Session 1. If you have any questions, contact your instructor.

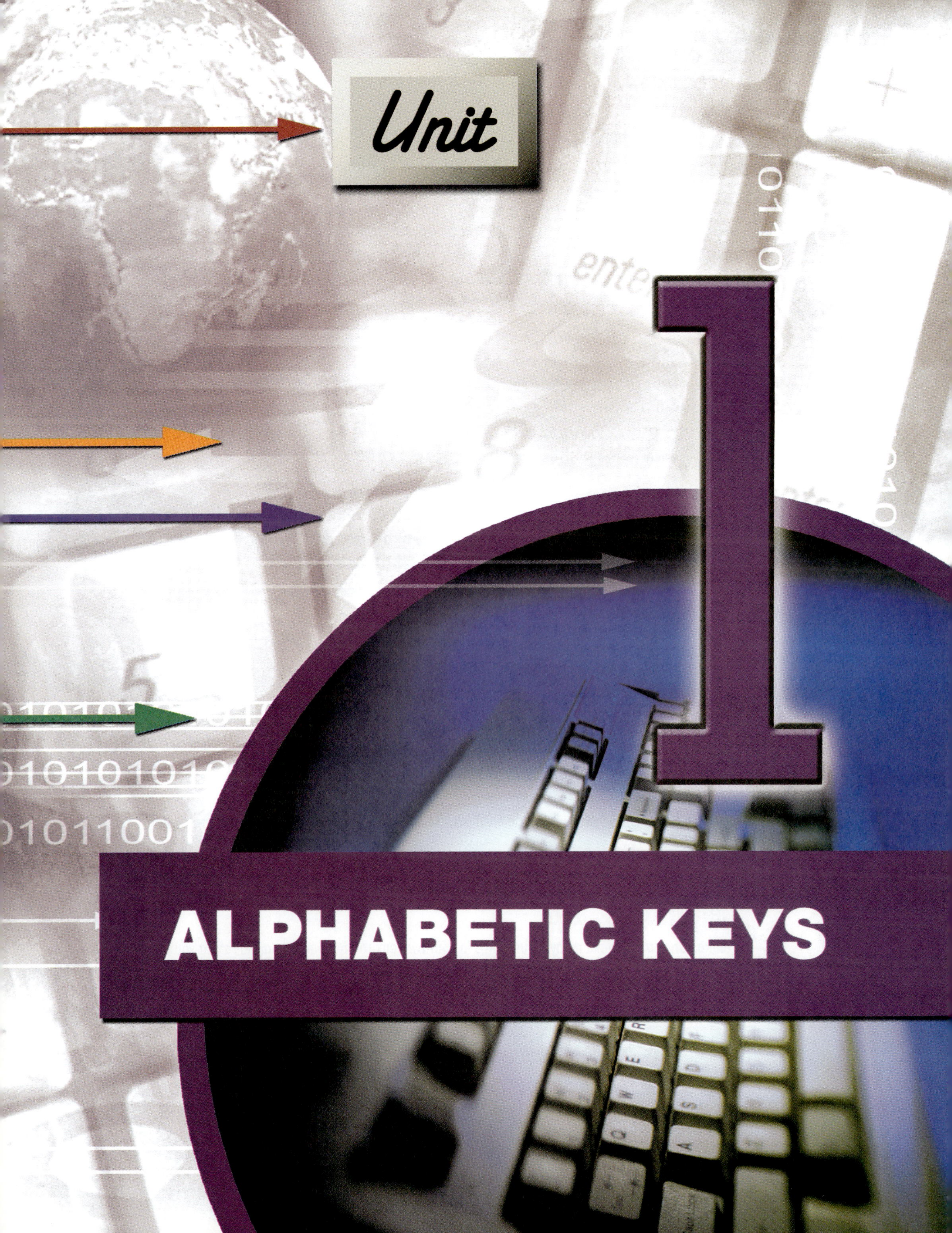
Unit
1
ALPHABETIC KEYS

30.6 FIVE-MINUTE TIMING

Goal: 25 WAM/2 errors

SI: 1.35

Take a 5-minute timing on the paragraphs that follow. If you complete the four paragraphs in less than five minutes, start over with the first paragraph and continue with paragraph 2, 3, and 4.

1 Most of the major events in communications grew out of a series of discoveries that took place over many years. Present-day systems can be traced to many great men and women who brought together the tools of their day to meet the needs of people on the job and in the home. The basis of this technology had its start in the 1830s.

One of the first events occurred in Germany when their government built a telegraph network that spanned 8,000 feet. By the next decade, the use of this device had spread to the United States. Congress funded a line that ran from Washington to Baltimore. During the same time frame, Samuel F.B. Morse finished a new telegraph device and code that came to be known as the Morse Code.

In the next few years, more developments took place. European telegraph wires and underwater cables became widely used. While the telegraph would continue to be used for many more years, other types of technology were taking shape. Bell developed the telephone in 1875, and he and Gray filed for a patent the next year. Bell later offered to sell his patents to Western Union, but they turned him down.

By the late 1880s, there were 140,000 homes in the U.S. with telephone service. The growth of this system has been impressive. Today there are 200 million lines that reach 93 percent of the homes in the U.S. The copper wire that has been used for so many years is being replaced by fiber optic cable that will bring voice, data, and video into our homes.

Ending the Session

Now you may print this session's files, continue to the next session, or exit the program. See page 118 of Session 28 if you need to review procedures.

Ergonomic Tip

Remember, you can make many adjustments in your own environment at little or no cost to you or your employer.

HOME ROW, SPACE BAR, ENTER

Session Goals

ASDF JKL;
Space Bar, Enter Key

1.1 On-Screen Exercises: Getting Started

You will be using the Paradigm Keyboarding with Snap (PKB) Web-based software along with your textbook to do the exercises that will help you develop your keyboarding skills.

To access PKB, take the following steps:

1. Log on to the Internet if your computer is not already connected to it.
2. At the Windows desktop of your computer, double-click the *Internet Explorer* icon.
3. At the Internet Explorer screen, click on the entry in the Address text box.
4. Key **www.keyboarding.emcp.com** in the Address text box and click *GO*. The Paradigm Keyboarding with Snap home page appears.

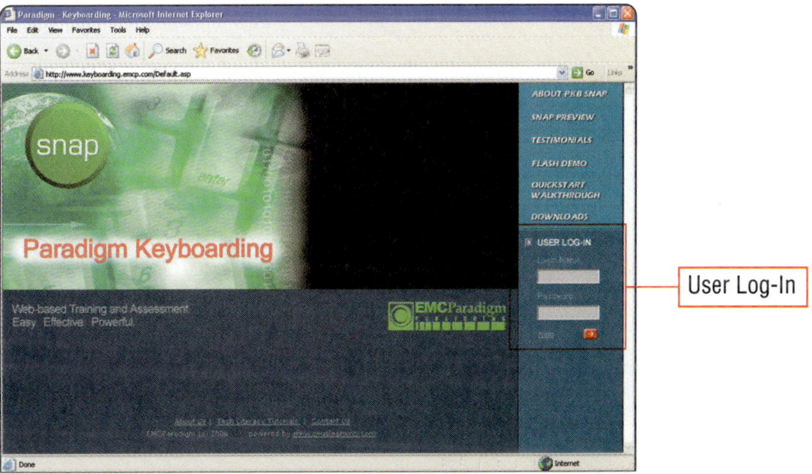

5. Your instructor has given you a Login Name that has been assigned for your class. The textbook package for your course includes a *Paradigm Keyboarding with Snap User Guide*. On the inside front cover of the *User Guide* is your unique PKB Password that you will use with the Login Name from your instructor to access PKB. Enter your login name in the Login Name text box (lower right corner of the screen). Enter your password in the Password text box.
6. Click the arrow in the red box.
7. When you log into Paradigm Keyboarding for the first time, you will be asked to read and agree to the Paradigm Keyboarding End User License Agreement, and to verify certain details about your course. You will need to do this only once.

A topic sentence expresses the main idea or subject of the paragraph. The topic sentence usually opens the paragraph, since most readers like to know what the paragraph is about before they read on. The topic sentence is bolded in the following example. **Supporting sentences** describe, explain, or further develop the topic sentence, as in this paragraph:

> **In a small office, the receptionist has a wide variety of duties.** Answering the telephone and receiving callers are primary responsibilities of any receptionist. Sometimes an employer asks a receptionist to take an important client to lunch or to contact a business customer. The correspondence in a small office varies from simple letters to complicated reports, and so the receptionist handles many types of communication.

Now, compose a paragraph about how you will use your keyboarding skills.

30.4 ONE-MINUTE TIMINGS

Goal: 35 WAM/2 errors

SI: 1.35

Take two 1-minute timings on the following paragraph.

> 1 At sunset, it is nice to enjoy dining out on a bank of a pond. Unless uninvited insects and swarms of ants invade the picnic, you will certainly unwind. As those soft night sounds enfold you, frenzied inward nerves and the decisions that haunt you drain from your mind. You may enjoy napping on a nearby bench. Next, swing into action after your rest and inhale much air into your lungs. Unpack the nice lunch and munch away. Don't deny yourself this experience.

30.5 THREE-MINUTE TIMINGS

Goal: 30 WAM/2 errors

SI: 1.39

Take two 3-minute timings on the following paragraph. If you complete the paragraph in less than three minutes, start over.

> 1 Simple salt and pepper shakers are very easy and quite simple to collect today. Lots of "fun" and very colorful pairs are available, either new or pre-owned. The bargains can be found at those family or group sales. Most folks try to see how many kinds they can find and buy. Some collect a mass of shakers that number over 500. The person or persons who are really collectors have shakers that number from 2,000 to 3,000 pairs. If anyone would like to begin the hobby of collecting, just look around and start a collection.

If the information displayed at this point is correct, click the Proceed button to continue.

8 Your Paradigm Keyboarding with Snap Welcome page appears.

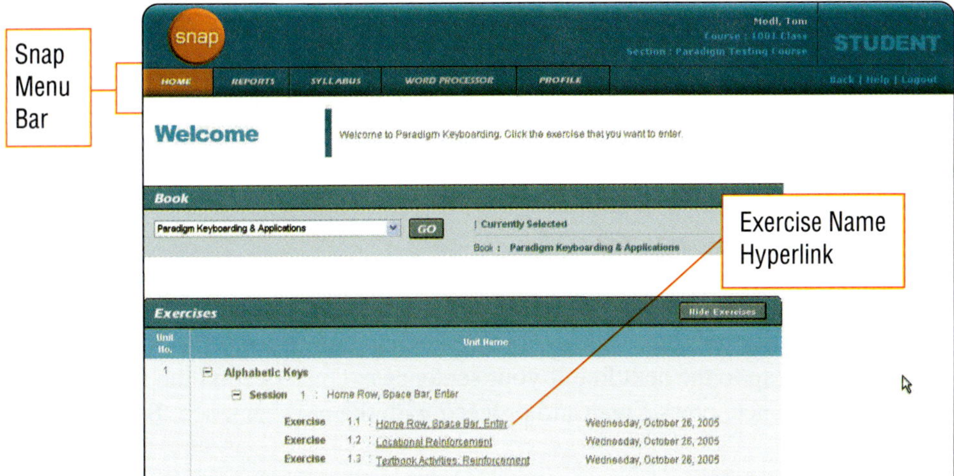

Find Exercise 1.1 in the Exercises table, and click Home Row, Space Bar, Enter. The Launch Keyboarding dialog box appears.

9 Click the Launch button.

10 The PKB Exercise screen appears.

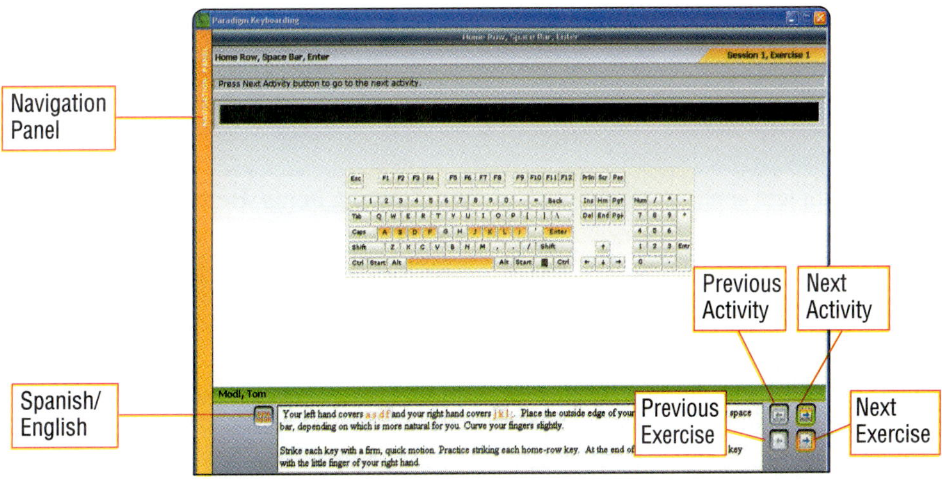

The PKB Exercise screen features the following buttons and functions:

Next Activity/Previous Activity These buttons take you to the next or previous activity within an exercise.

Next Exercise/Previous Exercise These buttons take you to the next or previous exercise of the program. These will provide the most common way of moving through the program.

Navigation Panel This feature allows you to move to any exercise within the program. Click on the orange panel with your mouse and a tree menu showing all the sessions and exercises in the program appears.

Spanish/English This toggle button allows you to view most software instructions in Spanish. Click the button to see instructions in Spanish. Click it again to see them in English.

Follow the instructions on screen to to complete Exercises 1.1 through 1.2. When you complete Exercise 1.2, Locational Reinforcement, there will be a message on the screen to return to page 4 in the text to complete Exercise 1.3, Textbook Reinforcement.

11 (Accept, Except) for Henry, the entire class went on the trip.
12 Our teacher strongly (adviced, advised) us to study for the exam.
13 There have been (fewer, less) absences this winter than last winter.
14 We have (fewer, less) flour than we need.
15 He is a (good, well) student.
16 Martha doesn't feel (good, well) today.
17 Sean plays the violin (good, well).
18 I am angry (at, about, with) my best friend.
19 I am angry (at, about, with) the rising costs of the textbooks.
20 I am angry (at, about, with) Whiskers, my cat.

Compose a complete sentence about each of the following items. Be sure to key the sentence number, period, and press the ***Tab*** key before keying your response. Let the sentence automatically wrap to the next line if your sentence extends beyond the right margin. At the end of each sentence, press ***Enter*** and proceed with the next sentence. Be sure to correct any errors.

1 ballpoint pen
2 ice cream
3 gas station
4 bank
5 elevator
6 fire
7 gain
8 dance
9 apple
10 water

Compose a complete sentence about each of the following items. Be sure to correct errors.

1 mirror
2 television
3 dollar bill
4 door
5 chair
6 radio
7 shoe
8 building
9 sunset
10 clock

Now you are ready to move on to the paragraph-response level, the fourth stage in building composition skills. Read the following guidelines for composing paragraphs. Study the guidelines and apply them in your composition activities.

General Guidelines for Paragraph Response

A paragraph is a group of related sentences—an organized and meaningful unit in a piece of writing. A paragraph contains a topic sentence and several supporting sentences. The sentences are organized in a logical manner and flow from one to the next. Transitional words connect one paragraph to another.

Textbook Exercises: Reinforcement

Welcome back! You have begun building your skill on the home keys, space bar, and Enter key. Everything you have keyed so far has been saved automatically in a file named 001ses. Now you will review the Session 1 keys.

Reviewing the Home Row Keys

Fingers

- Left hand on ASDF
- Right hand on JKL;
- Either left or right thumb on space bar
- Little finger of right hand for Enter

Students in Online Classes:

Whether working from the screen or text, keep your eyes on the copy; this will help you build speed.

Home Row Drill

- Key each line once.
- Keep eyes on copy.
- Press ***Enter*** at the end of each line. Press ***Enter*** twice between groups of lines.
- Repeat any group of 3 lines if you need more practice.

1 aaa sss ddd fff jjj kkk lll ;;; sd kl ;
2 aa ss dd ff jj kk ll ;; asdf jkl; af j;
3 a s d f j k l ; aa ss dd ff jj kk ll ;;

4 a ad a ad add add adds adds a ad add ad
5 a as as a ask ask asks asks a all all a
6 ad add as ask a; a; as adds asks a;; ad

7 fads fads fall fall falls falls fad fad
8 lass lass lad lad lads dad dads ask ask
9 falls flask alas fads dads asks all sad

Drill

Key the following drill. Press ***Enter*** after each line.

1 all all
2 sad sad dad dad

3 fad fad alas alas
4 fall fall lad lad add add

2 **Use English idioms correctly.** An idiom is an expression peculiar to a culture and is perfectly acceptable if used correctly.

Examples:

Correct	*Incorrect*	*Correct*	*Incorrect*
acquitted of	acquitted from	in search of	in search for
aim to prove	aim at proving	kind of (+ noun)	kind of a (+ noun)
can't help feeling	can't help but feel	aloud	out loud
comply with	comply to	try to	try and
independent of	independent from	different from	different than

3 **Use the correct word;** the words shown below are often misused.

Examples:

accept *to take or receive*	except *to leave out; aside from*
advice *a recommendation*	advise *to recommend*
biannual *twice a year*	biennial *once every two years*
council *a governing body*	counsel *to give advice*
fewer *(use with nouns that can be counted: fewer apples)*	less *(use with nouns that cannot be counted: less noise)*
good *modifies a noun or pronoun*	well *modifies a verb or adverb*
angry at *(things and animals)*	angry with *(people)*
angry about *(occasions or situations)*	

Sentence Response

Drawing from your experience and observations, think of descriptive words or phrases to make the following five sentences more interesting. Then key the sentence number, a period, and press ***Tab*** (Indent) before keying your revised sentence. In sentences 6–20 select the correct word/phrase. After you have keyed all twenty sentences, correct any errors you made. If your sentence goes beyond the right margin, let word wrap work for you. At the end of each sentence, press ***Enter*** and continue with the next sentence.

For a review of how to correct errors, go to Session 4, page 17, "Correcting Errors Review." To reinforce proofreading techniques go to Session 7, page 27, "Common Keyboarding Errors."

1 The last book I read was good.
2 Today is a nice day.
3 My favorite sport is fun.
4 My favorite color is a nice color.
5 My best friend is nice.

Students in Online Classes

For sentences 1–5, key the number, period, space, and then key the sentence. Press the Enter key, Tab, and then key your entry. Press Enter. Proceed in the same manner for the remaining four sentences.

Select the correct idiom in the following sentences, and key each sentence using the correct words. Check the "General Guidelines for Correct Word Use" if you have a question about which alternative to use.

6 (Try to, Try and) key the data without any errors.
7 Juan went (in search for, in search of) a new printer ribbon.
8 My book is (different from, different than) Harriet's book.
9 I will try to (comply with, comply to) your wishes.
10 This (kind of a, kind of) paper is easier to store.

Select the correct word in the following sentences, and key each sentence using the correct word.

Additional Drill

Key the following drill. Press ***Enter*** after each line.

1 a all all a alas alas a as ad add ask a
2 ask ask asks asks all all alas alas all

3 ad add as ask all alas adds asks all ad
4 dad dad dads dads sad sad fad fad fads
5 flak flak flask flask lad lad lads lads

Ending the Session

Now that you have completed this session, you have three options:

1. Print any documents you have created.
2. Continue with the next session.
3. Exit Snap Paradigm Keyboarding.

Print

To print Exercises 1.1 – 1.3 proceed as follows:

1. Click the Close button in the top right corner of the PKB Exercise screen.
2. At your Paradigm Keyboarding with Snap Welcome page, point to Reports on the Snap menu bar, and click View Submissions Report.
3. At the View Submissions Report Wizard, click Show session files.
4. Click Show Report.
5. Click 001ses.rtf.
6. At the Word Processor dialog box, click Launch.
7. Click File, and then click Print.
8. At the Print dialog box, click OK.
9. Click the Close button to close the Paradigm Word Processor.
10. Click Home on the Snap menu bar to return to the Welcome page.

Continue

To continue on the next session, click the Next Exercise button **twice**. This will take you to Exercise 2.2. (You will bypass Exercise 2.1 Warmup since you are already warmed up.)

Exit

To exit, do the following:

1. Click the Close button in the top right corner of the screen.
2. At your Paradigm Keyboarding with Snap Welcome page, click Logout.

Ergonomic Tip

Sit upright in your seat using back of the chair for lumbar support to eliminate lower back pain and strain.

Session 30

SENTENCE/PARAGRAPH RESPONSE

Session Goals

Compose sentence/paragraph levels
Choosing the right word

1-Minute: 35 WAM/2 errors
3-Minute: 30 WAM/2 errors
5-Minute: 25 WAM/2 errors

30.1-30.2 On-Screen Exercises: Getting Started

If you exited the program at the end of the previous session, refer to page 114 of Session 28 to review how to open the next session or to continue from where you left off.

30.3 Textbook Exercises: Reinforcement

This section offers more composition activities that include a review of correct word use. When you have finished these activities, click Print (if desired), then Next Exercise.

Choosing the Right Word

One of the most common problems a writer faces is choosing the correct word to convey a certain thought or idea to the reader. Writing must be precise; vague words or the misuse of words may change the author's meaning. Review the "General Guidelines for Correct Word Use" that follow. Keep them in mind as you key responses in the composing drills.

General Guidelines for Correct Word Use

1 **Use concrete nouns and descriptive adjectives, adverbs, and phrases; do not use vague or abstract words.** Vague words can mean many different things. Words such as **nice, good, bad, thing,** and **work** do not give the reader much information. Read each of the following and notice the differences.

Examples:

Vague:	The lecture was good, and I learned a lot.
Better:	The lecture solved two problems for me. I learned how to balance a checkbook and how to calculate interest.
Vague:	a nice color
Better:	an emerald green, a vivid scarlet, a dull black
Vague:	he said
Better:	he shouted defiantly, he muttered, he demanded.

Right Shift, H, E
Correcting errors, Backspace, Insert, Delete

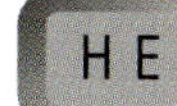

Right Shift, H, E, Backspace, Insert, Delete

Correcting errors with Backspace, Overtype, and Delete

2.1–2.5 On-Screen Exercises: Getting Started

If you exited Snap Paradigm Keyboarding at the end of Session 1, proceed as follows:

1. At the Windows desktop, double-click the *Internet Explorer* icon.
2. At the Internet Explorer screen, click on the entry in the Address text box.
3. Key **www.keyboarding.emcp.com** and click *GO*.
4. At the Paradigm Keyboarding with Snap page, enter your login name in the Login Name text box (lower right corner of the screen). Enter the password from your User Guide in the Password text box.
5. Click the arrow in the red box.
6. Your Paradigm Keyboarding with Snap Welcome page appears. Go to Exercise 2.1 and click Warmup.
7. The Launch Keyboarding dialog box appears; click the Launch button. Follow the instructions on the screens to complete Exercises 2.1 through 2.5.
8. When you complete Exercise 2.5, Locational Reinforcement, there will be a message on the screen to return to page 6 in the text to complete Exercise 2.6, which is a review of what has been presented in the software.

2.6 Textbook Exercises: Reinforcement

With a clear editing window displayed, you will now key drill lines you keyed earlier along with some new ones. This activity will be a reinforcement and review of the key reaches presented in Exercises 2.2–2.5. In addition, you will learn several ways to correct errors.

Correcting Errors

Here are three ways to correct any keying errors you might make as you complete Reinforcement activities:

Backspace: deletes characters as you backspace over them.

Overtype: replaces text letter by letter at the insertion point position. This feature is turned on and off when you press ***Insert***. (This is referred to as a toggle key.)

Delete: deletes character at the insertion point position.

1 Taking photos with a good camera can be fun. Most photo equipment has some method of setting a variety of focal lengths. A focal length setting of 35mm gives a wider picture angle, and it can be used for group portraits or photos of landscapes. A focal length setting of 70mm has a narrow angle for making a portrait or taking a good photo of a good scene or object that is far away. Using the zoom lens requires some practice before a picture can be a work of art.

29.6 FIVE-MINUTE TIMING

Goal: 25 WAM/2 errors

SI: 1.29

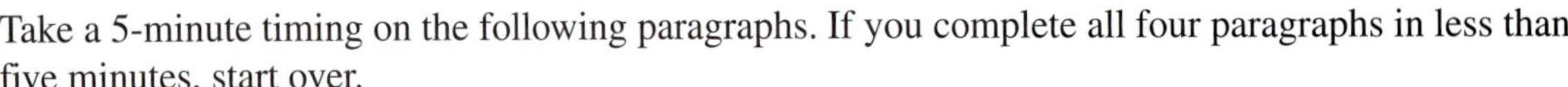

Take a 5-minute timing on the following paragraphs. If you complete all four paragraphs in less than five minutes, start over.

1 Education has become a lifelong process. No longer can we say that a person's formal schooling will last for a lifetime. Business spends almost as much for training programs as is spent for our public school system. The average age of students in schools offering programs above the high school level is on the rise.

Adult learners enter school programs with needs and wants that differ from the requirements of traditional students. They are goal-oriented. They are looking for skills and knowledge that will help them keep a job, prepare for a new job, or advance to a higher-level job. Adults don't want to waste time in reaching new skills; they want to spend their time on those things that relate to their goals.

Teachers and trainers of adult learners are faced with a tough task. In most cases, they must narrow the focus of their programs to meet the needs of the learners. Courses must be designed that draw upon the learners' skills and knowledge. To design a good program, you must assess what the learners know and what their goals are.

The next step in the process is to design a performance outcome that shows that the person can demonstrate a mastery of what was presented in the course. Once the outcome has been set, the instructor can choose teaching methods, course length, texts needed, and program content. Problem-solving, learn by doing, and case studies are methods of teaching that help adult students.

ENDING THE SESSION

Now you may print this session's files, continue to the next session, or exit the program. See page 118 of Session 28 if you need to review procedures.

Ergonomic Tip

Sit up straight, drop your shoulders back, and let your arms and hands hang loosely. This takes the strain off your back and allows your lungs and other organs to function correctly.

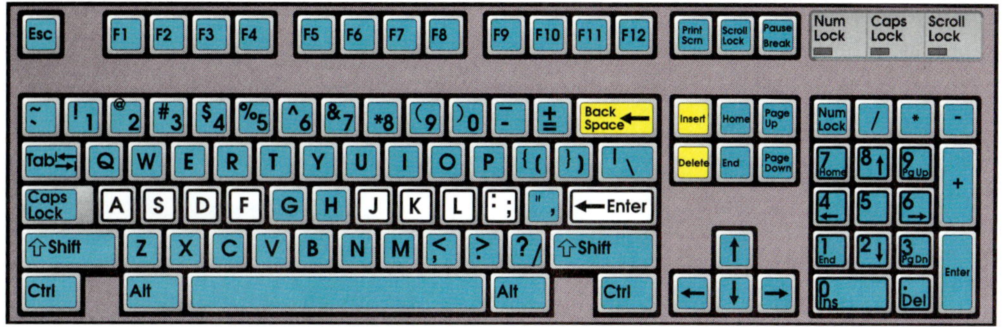

Correcting with Backspace

Move the insertion point to the right of the letter you want to correct. Press the Backspace key to delete the letter, then key the correct letter. To practice correcting with the Backspace key, do the following:

1. Key **saf**.
2. Press the Backspace key to delete f.
3. Key the letter **d**.
4. Press the space bar, then key **lasd**.
5. Press the Backspace key to delete the d.
6. Key the letter **s**.
7. Press the space bar, then key **flasd**.
8. Press the Backspace key to delete d.
9. Key the letter **k**. Press ***Enter***.

Your line should now look like this:

sad lass flask

Correcting with Overtype

By default, Overtype is off. This means that anything you key is inserted in the text rather than keyed over existing text. If you want to insert or add text, leave Overtype off. If, however, you want to key over something, turn Overtype on by pressing the ***Insert*** key. Overtype stays in effect until you press the ***Insert*** key again.

To practice correcting with the Overtype feature, do the following:

1. Key the following line:

   Sad All Asks Dads Fads Alas Flask Falls

2. Press the ***Insert*** key.
3. Change the uppercase S in Sad to a lowercase s. To do this, move the insertion point with either the mouse or the left arrow key immediately left of the S and key **s**.
4. Change the remaining uppercase letters to lowercase.
5. Turn Overtype off by pressing the ***Insert*** key.

Your line should now look like this:

sad all asks dads fads alas flask falls

A hammer is used to ____________ .
A lawn mower is used to ____________ .
Scissors are used to ____________ .
A pencil is used to ____________ .
An eraser is used to ____________ .

Sentences

Read a question and then answer it by keying a complete sentence. Number each sentence. The first one is done as a sample. ***Remember:*** Do not hesitate. Key your answer as quickly as possible. Press ***Enter*** after each response.

What does a police officer do? A police officer enforces the laws.
What does a plumber do?
What does a firefighter do?
What does a lawyer do?
What does a teacher do?
What does an auto mechanic do?
What does a medical doctor do?
What does a dentist do?
What does an accountant do?
What does a chef do?

29.4 ONE-MINUTE TIMINGS

Goal: 35 WAM/2 errors

SI: 1.27

Take two 1-minute timings on the following paragraph.

1 The news on the network newscast might spawn a winning wealth of followers. If the newscaster can draw a wider range of viewers, the rewards are power and wealth. Watchers and followers of a witty newscaster are won when the daily news is written well. It is not a waste to rewrite the worst of interviews when witless words can wreck a well planned show or review. They who dawdle in the newsroom will not work or write very long. Their reward will be awful reviews.

29.5 THREE-MINUTE TIMINGS

Goal: 30 WAM/2 errors

SI: 1.33

Take two 3-minute timings on the following paragraph. If you complete the paragraph in less than three minutes, start over.

Correcting with Delete

When correcting with the Delete key, simply position the insertion point on or just to the left of the character to be deleted. Press the ***Delete*** key to remove the character, then key the correct letter.

To practice correcting with the Delete key, do the following:

1. Key the following line:

Fall Alas Sad Asksv

2. Position the insertion point on or just to left of a in Fall.
3. Press the ***Delete*** key.
4. Key **e**.
5. Position the insertion point on or just to left of the last s in Asks.
6. Press ***Delete***.

Your line should now look like this:

Fell Alas Sad Ask

Reviewing the Right Shift, H, and E Keys

Remember: The right Shift key is used to make capital letters that are keyed with the left hand.

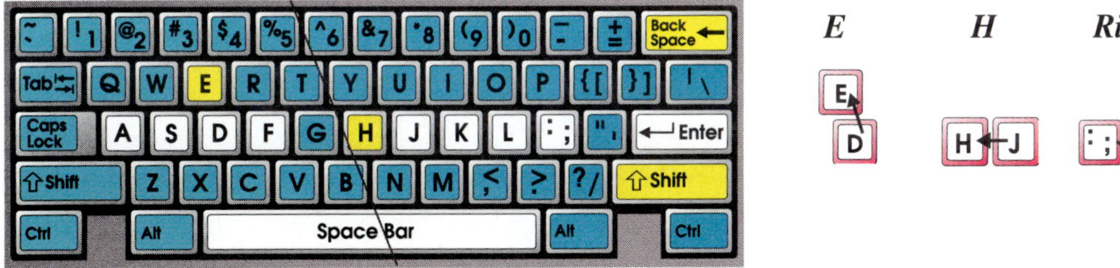

Drill Instructions

- Key each line once; keep your eyes on the copy.
- Press ***Enter*** at the end of each line.
- Key the appropriate group of lines again if you need more practice. Do not try to correct errors.

Right Shift Drill

1 Ad All Asks Adds Alas All Ask As Add Ad
2 Fad fad Falls falls Fall fall Fads fads
3 Sad All Asks Dads Fads Alas Flask Falls

2. a. What is your first and last name?
   b. What is your friend's first and last name?
   c. What is the title of your favorite song?
   d. What is the name of the last movie you saw?
   e. What is the name of the last television show you saw?

3. a. Where were you born?
   b. Where did you attend elementary school?
   c. Where did you go on your last vacation?
   d. Where are you going after class today?
   e. Where will you be tomorrow at this time?

4. a. What are your favorite sports?
   b. What are your favorite colors?
   c. What will you be doing five years from now?
   d. What is the name of your favorite class?
   e. What is the name of your best friend?

Longer Phrases

Think of a phrase that completes each sentence. Number each sentence, followed by a period, press Tab, and then key the sentence to include your response. There are 20 sentences in this group. Press ***Enter*** after each response.

Because the clock was wrong, I ____________ .
Because the road was icy, I ____________ .
Because the team won, I ____________ .
Because I was late, I ____________ .
Because I can/cannot drive, I ____________ . (Choose either can or cannot.)

If I pass this test, I ____________ .
If I finish early, I ____________ .
If I get the job, I ____________ .
If the price is right, I ____________ .
If the beach is crowded, I ____________ .

I do/do not like loud music because ____________ .
I do/do not study at the library because ____________ .
I do/do not obey the speed limit because ____________ .
I do/do not like math because ____________ .
I do/do not play sports because ____________ .

H Drill

1 jh hall hall hall sash sash has sash hash
2 half half half lash lash lash half lash
3 Dads sash Falls Shall Shall Flash Flash

Whether pushing for speed or control, at this point do not stop to correct errors.

E Drill

Key lines 1–2 once for speed; try to make your fingers go faster.

1 deal dead deaf fade seat led lead lease lake
2 she she ale ale elf elf elk elk heat heat fake fake

Key lines 3–5 once for control; slow down and concentrate on control.

3 deal deal ease ease else else desk desk fell fell
4 fade fade feel feel dead dead head head heal heal
5 Elk Elk Else Ease Ed Elf Else Ease Ed Ed

Additional Drill

Key the following drill. Press ***Enter*** after each line.

1 half half
2 flash flash shall shall
3 fall hall alas dash half
4 lad lad lads lads Flak Flak Flask Flask

5 Sad Dad Add Ask Fad Salad Flak Dads All
6 Dads Ask lad Ask dad lads lass lass Add
7 jh has had has had has had has had lash
8 ha has ash Ash Ash had ash ash hall Flash

9 eel deed eel she see she see ale elf ale fee
10 ease deal ease deal else desk else desk fell
11 fade feel fade feel dead head dead head heal
12 Else Elk Ease Ed Elf Else Ease Ed Elf Ed

Session 29

PHRASE/SENTENCE RESPONSE

Session Goals

Compose at Phrase-Response Level

1-Minute: 35 WAM/2
3-Minute: 30 WAM/2 errors
5-Minute: 25 WAM/2 errors

29.1-29.2 On-Screen Exercises: Getting Started

If you exited the program at the end of the previous session, refer to page 114 of Session 28 to review how to open the next session or to continue from where you left off.

29.3 Textbook Exercises: Reinforcement

In this section you will continue learning to think and compose at the keyboard. You will practice keying whole phrases and sentences in response to questions offered in the following drills. When you have finished the drills, click Print (if desired), then click Next Exercise.

Composing Phrases

Now that you have completed the word-response level, you can move on to the phrase-response level and sentence-response level. At a clear editing window, read the questions and then answer them by keying the question number, period, one space; then press ***Tab***, key the letter, a period, one space, then the answer. Press ***Enter*** and go to the next question. For the second and remaining questions in each group, just press ***Tab***, then key the letter, a period, one space, and the answer. Press ***Enter*** after each response. Do not make complete sentences—just answer the question. If you do not know the correct answer, invent one. ***Remember:*** Do not hesitate. Key your answer as quickly as possible.

Short Phrases

1. a. What is the name of a town and state/province that you would like to visit?
   b. What is your instructor's first and last name?
   c. What is the president's/prime minister's last name?
   d. What is the name of this book?
   e. What is the name of this course?

For Groups 1–4, after keying the letter and period, enter a space, then key each question followed by a question mark. Enter a space, then key the phrase for your response.

Ending the Session

At the end of each session, you have three options:

- Print any documents you have created.
- Continue with the next session.
- Exit Paradigm Keyboarding with Snap.

Print

To print Exercises 2.1 – 2.6 proceed as follows:

1. Click the Close button in the top right corner of the screen.
2. At your Paradigm Keyboarding with Snap Welcome page, point to Reports on the Snap menu bar, and click View Submissions Report.
3. At the View Submissions Report Wizard, click Show session files.
4. Click Show Report.
5. Click 002ses.rtf.
6. At the Word Processor dialog box, click Launch.
7. Click File, and then click Print.
8. At the Print dialog box, click OK.
9. Click the Close button to close the Paradigm Word Processor.
10. Click Home on the Snap menu bar to return to the Welcome page.

Continue

To continue on the next session, click the Next Exercise button **twice**. This will take you to Exercise 3.2. (You will bypass Exercise 3.1 Warmup since you are already warmed up.)

Exit

To exit, do the following:

1. Click the Close button in the top right corner of the screen.
2. At your Paradigm Keyboarding with Snap Welcome page, click Logout.

Ergonomic Tip

Press keys lightly and do not use pressure when keying.

Continue

To continue on the next session, click the Next Exercise button. This will take you to Exercise 29.1.

Exit

To exit, do the following steps:

1 Click the Close button in the top right corner of the screen.
2 At your Paradigm Keyboarding with Snap Welcome page, click Logout.

Ergonomic Tip

Take small breaks as short as 10 seconds every 30 minutes to stretch; this will help you relax and relieve tension.

Session 3 PERIOD, T, COMMA, CAPS LOCK

Session Goals

Period, T, Comma, Caps Lock

Descriptive Words

3.1–3.6 ## On-Screen Exercises: Getting Started

If you exited Snap Paradigm Keyboarding at the end of Session 2, proceed as follows:

1. At the Windows desktop, double-click the *Internet Explorer* icon.
2. At the Internet Explorer screen, click on the entry in the Address text box.
3. Key **www.keyboarding.emcp.com** and click *GO*.
4. At the Paradigm Keyboarding with Snap page, enter your login name in the Login Name text box (lower right corner of the screen). Enter your password in the Password text box.
5. Click the arrow in the red box.
6. Your Paradigm Keyboarding with Snap Welcome page appears. Go to Exercise 3.1 and click Warmup.
7. The Launch Keyboarding dialog box appears; click the Launch button. Follow the instructions on the screens to complete Exercises 3.1 through 3.6.
8. When you complete Exercise 3.6, Locational Reinforcement, there will be a message on the screen to return to page 11 in the text to complete Exercise 3.7, which is a review of what has been presented in the software.

3.7 ## Textbook Exercises: Reinforcement

In this activity, you will review the key reaches and activities presented in Exercises 3.2–3.6.

Reviewing the Period, T, Comma, and Caps Lock Keys

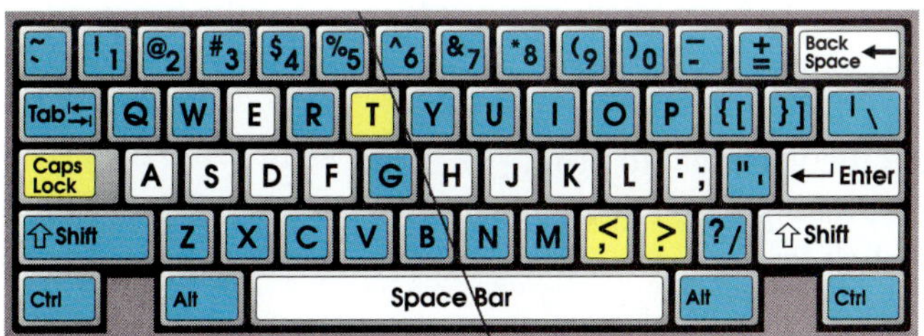

Caps Lock *T* *Comma* *Period*

28.6 FIVE-MINUTE TIMING

Goal: 25 WAM/2 errors

SI: 1.29

Take a 5-minute timing on the following paragraphs. If you finish the three paragraphs before the five minutes are up, start over with the first paragraph and continue.

1 The most important piece of furniture in an office is the chair. Workers will spend most of their day doing their work while seated. If people are uncomfortable, they will not be as productive as they could be with the right chair. It has been stated that a person's productivity will increase 15 to 20 percent when using a chair that fits his or her body.

There are several features to look for in selecting a chair to be used in an office setting. First, make sure it has a five-star base so that it won't tip over. Next, make sure that the seat adjusts upward and downward to fit the person using it. The back rest must be adjustable up and down so that it supports the worker's back. The front of the chair must have a "water fall," or downward-curved cushion, so that there is no pressure behind the knees while the worker is seated.

Any adjustments to be made to chair height, back support, or tilt must be easy to do. There are chairs on the market that adjust as the person sits down; no manual adjustments need to be made. Another important part of a chair is the covering. Some coverings are warm (they don't breathe). Chairs can be purchased with arms that drop so that the chair can be moved closer to the desk.

ENDING THE SESSION

Now you may print this session's files, continue to the next session, or exit the program.

Print

To print Exercises 28.1 – 28.6 proceed as follows:

1. Click the Close button in the top right corner of the screen.
2. At your Paradigm Keyboarding with Snap Welcome page, point to Reports on the Snap menu bar, and click View Submissions Report.
3. At the View Submissions Report Wizard, click Show session files to see the drill lines text (Exercises 28.1-28.3), or Show timings files to see the timings text (Exercises 28.4-28.6).
4. Click Show Report.
5. Click the name of the file you want to print.
6. At the Word Processor dialog box, click Launch.
7. Click File, and then click Print.
8. At the Print dialog box, click OK.
9. Click the Close button to close the Paradigm Word Processor.
10. Click Home on the Snap menu bar to return to the Welcome page.

Drill Instructions

- Key each line once.
- If you are not comfortable with a reach, repeat the appropriate group of two lines.

Period Drill

Important: Tap the space bar once after the period at the end of a sentence. Only one space is required when you use a proportionally spaced font such as the PKB default, Times New Roman. (Proportionally spaced means each character is designed relative to the other letters. The i, for example, is narrower than the t or the m. On the other hand, characters in monospaced fonts such as Courier each take up the same amount of space.)

For this text, unless instructed otherwise, enter one space after a period or other sentence-ending punctuation.

Note: If a period ends a line, press ***Enter*** immediately. There is no need to tap the space bar.

1 All lads shall dash. A lad shall fall.
2 Ask a sad lad. Sad lads fall. Ask Al.

T Drill

1 ft at hat hats sat sat tall tall data data
2 fast fast slat slat halt halt last last fat fat

Comma Drill

Remember: Do not space before a comma, but always space once after a comma (except when keying numbers).

1 That tall, fat, fast lad shall ask dad.
2 A flat, half lath falls; all lads halt.

Caps Lock Drill

Note: The little finger on the left hand reaches to press ***Caps Lock***.

1 STALK A FAST LAD; A SAD LAD HAS A FALL.
2 DAD HALTS A TALL LAD. A SAD LAD HALTS.

Note: Tap the Caps Lock key to return to lower case.

f. stop
g. no
h. winter
i. sick
j. True

Syllabic Intensity

Beginning with this session, the **syllabic intensity** (the average number of syllables per word) is listed for all 1-, 3-, and 5-minute timings. Syllabic intensity (SI) is an approximate indication of how difficult material is to key. The lower the SI, the easier the material is to key; the higher the SI, the more difficult the material, since the words are longer.

When you take timings, your goal is to improve either your speed or your accuracy. You must concentrate on one or the other. Your goal will probably change daily—or even during a particular class period. Note that with this session, the speed goals for the 1- and 3-minute timings have been raised by 5 WAM.

28.4 ONE-MINUTE TIMINGS

Goal: 35 WAM/2 errors

SI: 1.27

Take two 1-minute timings on the following paragraph.

1 Long ago, pilgrims loved to indulge in blunt folklore. Tales, sometimes false, were told with glee daily. One old tale included a blazing clash of sailors in balky sailboats on a bottomless lake. The last sailor alive was a lad that was blind. As he lay clinging to a slim balsa log in filth and slimy silt, the leader's falcon led help to him. Balmy days followed as the lad's leg healed slowly and the salves applied to his eyes let the light in.

28.5 THREE-MINUTE TIMINGS

Goal: 30 WAM/2 errors

SI: 1.33

Take two 3-minute timings on the following paragraph. If you complete the paragraph in less than three minutes, start over.

1 To change a U.S. unit of measure to a metric unit of measure takes practice and knowledge. To change back and forth, a table of metric measures and U.S. units of measures is great to have. For instance, 1 mile is equal to a metric measurement of 1.6 kilometers. One yard is about the same as a metric measure of 0.9 meters. One can change a larger metric unit to a smaller one by moving the decimal point one place to the right.

Building Speed

Your mind controls your fingers, so think **speed.** After you practice setting your "mind" goal several times, you should find that your mind eventually controls your fingers automatically.

Key lines 1–3 once. Key lines 1–3 again as fast as you can.

1 Stalk a fast lad; a sad lad has a hat.
2 A lad talks; the dad talks; a dad talks.
3 Dad halts the sad lad. A sad lad halts.

Students in Online Classes

Key each group of three lines twice; push for speed while keeping your eyes on the copy. Do not correct errors.

Additional Drill

Key the following drill. Key each line once. If you find yourself hesitating, repeat the line. Press ***Enter*** after each line.

1 The lads dash. A dad asks the lads.
2 Feds dash. Dads dash. Dads ask the sad lads.
3 Ask Al. Sad lads halt. Ask a sad lad.

4 data data data slat slat slat jet jet jet
5 that that that task task talk talk talk
6 salt salt salt flat flat flat lath lath lath

7 A flat atlas; a flat hat; a flat flask.
8 A half a flask; a half lath; half a slat.
9 A sad lad halts. Dad halts a fat lad.

10 A sad lad has a hat. Stalk a fast lad.
11 A half lath; half a flask; half a slat.
12 The fat lads talked fast. A dad talks fast.

13 Dash, Al, Flat, half, lath, head, heat,
14 A fat, sad, flat, red hat has the lead.
15 Dale asked Al. Dad asked the lads.

Ending the Session

At the end of each session, you have three options:

- Print any documents you have created.
- Continue with the next session.
- Exit Paradigm Keyboarding with Snap.

2. a. Are you a female or a male?
   b. Are you right- or left-handed?
   c. Is the instructor of this class male or female?
   d. Would you rather drink milk or tea?
   e. Would you rather dance or read?

3. a. Would you rather dance or sing?
   b. Would you rather eat hot dogs or hamburgers?
   c. Would you rather write or read?
   d. Would you rather study or play?
   e. Would you rather own a dog or a cat?

4. a. Do you like summer or winter best?
   b. Would you rather be short or tall?
   c. Would you rather be dirty or clean?
   d. Would you rather win or lose?
   e. Would you rather run or walk?

Word Response: Opposites

Read a word and then key the word's opposite, using the same procedure you followed in the previous drills. If you cannot think of an opposite, key the word shown. Press ***Enter*** after each response. ***Remember:*** Do not hesitate. Key your answer as quickly as possible.

1. a. day
   b. salt
   c. mother
   d. uncle
   e. grandmother
   f. rich
   g. war
   h. young
   i. love
   j. hot

For Groups 1 and 2, after keying the letter and period, space once, key the word. Press tab and then key your one-word response. Do this for each of the words in the two groups.

2. a. clean
   b. male
   c. minus
   d. seldom
   e. floor

Print

To print Exercises 3.1 – 3.7 proceed as follows:

1. Click the Close button in the top right corner of the screen.
2. At your Paradigm Keyboarding with Snap Welcome page, point to Reports on the Snap menu bar, and click View Submissions Report.
3. At the View Submissions Report Wizard, click Show session files.
4. Click Show Report.
5. Click 003ses.rtf.
6. At the Word Processor dialog box, click Launch.
7. Click File, and then click Print.
8. At the Print dialog box, click OK.
9. Click the Close button to close the Paradigm Word Processor.
10. Click Home on the Snap menu bar to return to the Welcome page.

Continue

To continue on the next session, click the Next Exercise button **twice**. This will take you to Exercise 4.2. (You will bypass Exercise 4.1 Warmup since you are already warmed up.)

Exit

To exit, do the following:

1. Click the Close button in the top right corner of the screen.
2. At your Paradigm Keyboarding with Snap Welcome page, click Logout.

Ergonomic Tip

Keep the keyboard positioned so that the front edge is lower than the back so that the forearms are slightly raised and wrists straight.

Word Response: Yes or No

Key answers to the questions that follow. For the first question in each group, key the question number followed by a period, press ***Tab***, then key the letter followed by a period, one space, and either ***yes*** or ***no*** or ***not sure***. Press ***Enter*** and go to the next question. For the second and remaining questions in each group, just press ***Tab***, then key the letter and a period, one space, and then the answer. Press ***Enter*** after each response. ***Remember:*** Do not hesitate. Key your answer as quickly as possible.

1. a. Do you like the weather today?
   b. Do you like animals?
   c. Are you hungry?
   d. Do you read the newspaper?
   e. Would you like to go into politics?
   f. Do you participate in any sport?
   g. Do you like animals?
   h. Are you hungry?
   i. Do you read the newspaper?
   j. Do you watch television every day?

Students in Online Classes

For Groups 1 and 2, after keying the letter and period, space once, and key the question. Key a space after the question mark and then key your Yes, No, or Not Sure response. This will give you more practice keying the alphabetic characters.

2. a. Are you tired?
   b. Do you have any brothers?
   c. Do you have any sisters?
   d. Do you have a job?
   e. Are you a "good" speller?
   f. Are you going on vacation soon?
   g. Do you like English?
   h. Do you like coffee?
   i. Would you like to travel overseas?
   j. Do you like to cook?

Word Response: Which One?

Answer the following questions with one of the two choices or with the word ***neither***. Follow the same procedure you used in the first drill. Press ***Enter*** after each response. ***Remember:*** Do not hesitate. Key your answer as quickly as possible.

1. a. Would you rather ski or swim?
   b. Would you rather drive or ride?
   c. Would you rather eat or cook?
   d. Would you rather walk or talk?
   e. Would you rather hike or bike?

Students in Online Classes

For Groups 1–4, after keying the letter and period, space once, and key the question. Key a space after the question mark and then your response.

N, LEFT SHIFT, COLON
Review of Correcting Errors

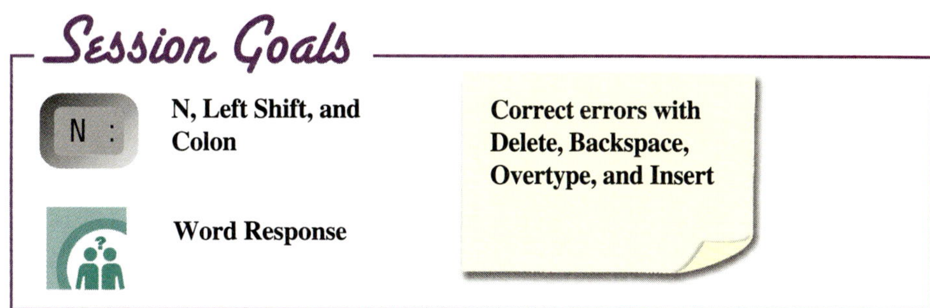

4.1–4.8 On-Screen Exercises: Getting Started

If you are continuing immediately from Session 3, you are already warmed up and are looking at Exercise 4.2. Click the Next Exercise button or Previous Exercise button if you are not at the correct exercise.

If you exited the program at the end of the previous session, refer to page 11 of Session 3 for instructions on entering the program.

4.9 Textbook Exercises: Reinforcement

Some of the drills you completed in Exercises 4.2–4.8 are repeated here, along with some new ones, to reinforce your keyboarding skills. You will also review error correction methods. When you have finished the Exercises in Session 4, click Print (if desired), click Next Exercise twice to continue with Exercise 5.2, or click the Close button to exit the program.

Building Keyboarding Speed

To increase your keyboarding skills, you must key without watching your fingers. Concentrate on keeping your eyes on the copy whether from the screen or text. When asked to key at a controlled rate or for accuracy, concentrate on making the correct reaches. When pushing for speed, concentrate on making your fingers move faster.

Reviewing the N, Left Shift, and Colon Keys

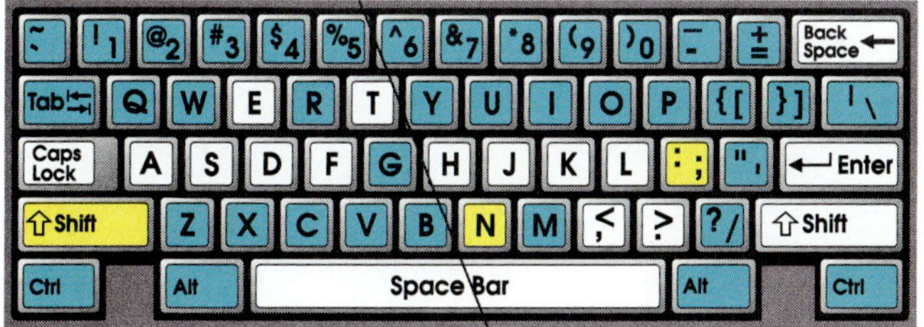

Left Shift

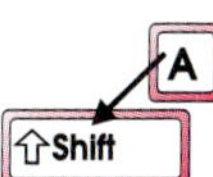

N

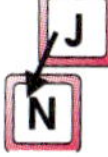

Session 28

WORD RESPONSE

Session Goals

Compose at Word-Response Level

1-Minute: 35 WAM/2 errors
3-Minute: 30 WAM/2 errors
5-Minute: 25 WAM/2 errors

28.1-28.2 On-Screen Exercises: Getting Started

If you are continuing immediately from Session 27, begin with Exercise 28.1. Click the Next Exercise or Previous Exercise button if you are not at the correct exercise.

If you exited the program at the end of the previous session, refer to page 11, Session 3 for instructions on entering the program.

28.3 Textbook Exercises: Reinforcement

This section provides practice in thinking and composing at the keyboard. Mastering this skill will speed up your preparation of documents. When you have finished this section, click Print (if desired), then Next Exercise.

Composing at the Keyboard

Now that you have learned the keyboard and have developed your skills further, it is time to learn to think and compose at the keyboard so you can use a computer efficiently.

There are four stages in building composition skills:

1. Developing skill at the **word-response** level. (You already began working at this level when you keyed the Thinking Drills.)
2. Developing skill at the **phrase-response** level.
3. Developing skill at the **sentence-response** level.
4. Developing skill at the **paragraph,** or "**complete,**" level.

N Drill

Students in Online Classes

Think speed as you key each line once—keep your eyes on the copy. Do not correct errors.

Key lines 1–2 once; push for speed.

1 an an and and land land sand sand tanks
2 slant slant thank thank and and ant ant

Key lines 3–5 once for control. If you make more than two errors on a line, repeat it.

3 Jan shall hand a sad lad an atlas fast.
4 Hal shall thank that tall and lank lad.
5 Hats and sandals shall stand as a fad.

Left Shift and Colon Drill

- Shift of semi (;) key produces a colon (:)
- When keying documents, press the space bar once after keying a colon.

1 jJ kK lL ;: Jj Kk Ll ;: JL; jK lL :;:; KL: hH:
2 Had; Lad; Has; Lass; Half: Lads: Hall: Jade:
3 Lass Lad Lads Head: Halt: Lead: Lads: Jet:

Additional Drill

Key the following drill. Press ***Enter*** after each line. If you find yourself hesitating when keying a line, repeat it.

1 land land than than flank flank tan tan slant slant
2 thank thank nasal nasal and Fan Fan Stand Stand
3 A tan shaft lands and halts that task.

4 As a fad, hats and sandals shall stand the sand.
5 Sal, Dan, and Dana ran and talked fast.
6 flash: flash: half: half: nail: nail: hand: hand:

7 Jean leased the tan hats, red jeans, and sandals.
8 Handle the jar that leaks; taste the lean tea.
9 She landed at a nest. The fat hen left the lake.
10 He felt tense. The ten lads and dad halted a theft.

Unit
5
COMPOSITION

Correcting Errors: Review

There are four ways to correct any keyboarding errors you make:

Backspace	When you backspace over a character on the screen, the character is deleted.
Delete	Press the ***Delete*** key to erase the character immediately right of the insertion point position.
Overtype	This function allows you to replace, or *type over,* existing text. To use Overtype, press the ***Insert*** key. The Overtype mode stays in effect until you press ***Insert*** again.
Insert	When you want to insert letters that were left out of a word, move the insertion point to the location where the first character will be added. Key the characters to be added.

To practice the correction methods, go to line 3 in the previous N drill (page 16) and change *Jan* to *Dan.* In line 4 insert *At last* at the beginning of the sentence and delete *and lank lad,* replacing it with *lass.*

Ending the Session

At this point, you may print this session's files, continue to the next session, or exit the program. See page 13 of Session 3 if you need to review procedures.

Ergonomic Tip

Use only finger, not wrist, movements to strike keys.

1 The population of the United States has become more varied culturally. It is extremely important that individuals be made aware of the need to communicate with other cultures in ways that are satisfying to both parties. As people interact on a daily basis, meanings are discovered that form a bond for common understanding.

2 The first thing a visitor notices at the travel agency is a bronze statue of the founder. The agency is merging with another travel group that will give them 4,000 office locations in 125 countries. The merger of their business and information systems will take five years.

Ending the Session

Now you may print this session's files, continue to the next session, or exit the program. See page 103 of Session 24 if you need to review procedures.

Ergonomic Tip

Slowly lift shoulders while inhaling, and then slowly drop shoulders while exhaling; this will help you relax.

I, G
Using Tab Defaults and Word Wrap

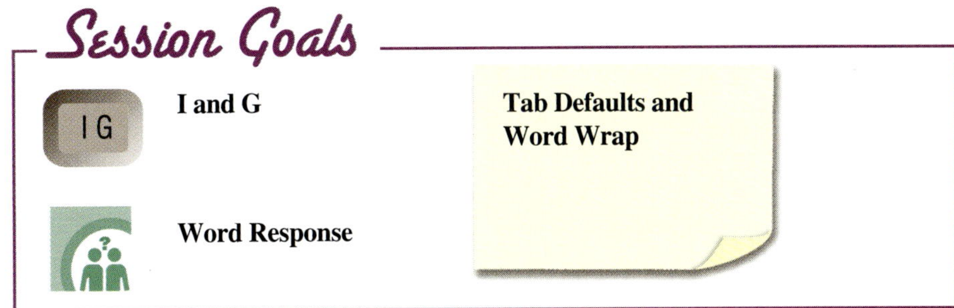

5.1-5.8

On-Screen Exercises: Getting Started

If you are continuing immediately from Session 4, you are already warmed up and are looking at Exercise 5.2. Click the Next Exercise or Previous Exercise button if you are not at the correct exercise.

If you exited the program at the end of the previous session, refer to page 11 of Session 3 for instructions on entering the program.

Textbook Exercises: Reinforcement

Now you will review the key reaches and activities completed in Exercises 5.2–5.8 The new material includes practice with using word wrap and tab defaults. When you have finished this exercise, click Print (if desired), click Next Exercise twice to continue with Exercise 6.2, or click the Close button to exit the program.

Reviewing the I and G Keys

G

I

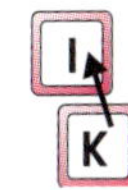

I Drill

Key lines 1–2 once; push for speed.

1 if if in in it it kid kid his fail fine file find
2 The kid thinks I had the idea that he did finish.

7 Send me 13 of Item 4 and 7 of Item 9 immediately.
8 West Arn 20 lb. paper has 99 percent rag content.
9 I have: 360 holders, 75 pencils, and 99 punches.

Additional Drill

Key the following drill for control on the 10-key numeric keypad. Press ***Enter*** after each line.

1 654 54 76 56 46 767 46 654 6054 567 7655 6054 456
2 687 577 575 876 754 796 697 757 885 855 644 54 66
3 78 81 8687 782 8422 789 987 432 8282 6732 321 989

4 08 080 797 580 680 4986 7984 47782 78853 88795 85
5 19105 05084 88 384 18 682 9764 7976 8828 55130 56
6 66938 88282 775 993 5549 7970 2810 82 879 8322087

7 10.18 7.85 8.94 15.63 40.38 .89 95.93 24.56 67.36 3.69
8 7.8 67.8 67.21 478.231 123.456 1.456 14.567 89.90 .65
9 4.8 21.6 41.72 687.452 4.872 48.729 72.94 729.45 65.8

At the end of each line proofread. If you have any errors, repeat the line until you can key it with out error before going to the next line.

27.4 TIMINGS: 10-KEY NUMERIC KEYPAD

Goal: 25 WAM with 0 errors

- Take a 1-minute timing on the lines in Group 1. Then take two 1-minute timings on the lines in Group 2.
- If you finish before time is up, start over.
- Press ***Tab*** with your "a" finger.
- Strike ***Enter*** at the end of each line.

1	12	34	56	78	90	123	456	789	987	654	321	4321
	98	76	54	32	10	321	654	897	978	456	123	1234
	76	89	32	12	01	789	564	987	654	545	231	2413
	54	12	12	34	28	897	546	978	123	466	132	1432
	32	54	78	56	58	978	645	789	101	654	213	2431

2	130	12.9	14.87	123.4	1.456	14.56	56.21	156.02	47
	8	67.8	67.21	478.23	2.789	27.879	87.90	879.08	56.49
	427	32.56	978.12	3.462	34.620	62.08	620.81	84.8	61
	72	687.45	4.872	48.729	72.94	729.45	25.2	52.5	98.12
	18724	9.678	96.78	8.69	687.89	2	672.3	598	390.26

27.5 TIMINGS: ALPHABETIC KEYS

Goal: 30 WAM with no more than 2 errors

Take a 1-minute timing on each paragraph.

Key lines 3–5 once at a controlled rate. If you make more than two errors on a line, repeat it.

3 Ill Inside Indeed If Illness Island Indeed Inside
4 She is a skilled athlete and likes little detail.
5 He did ski that hill. That is indeed a sad test.

G Drill

Key lines 1–2 once; push for speed.

1 gal gal gaxs gas get get sag sag egg egg gal gal
2 Dennis and Gene nailed a lath in the big red gate.

Key lines 3–5 once; concentrate on control—try not to make errors.

3 Giant Giggle Glide Gentle Gene Gain Gift Glad Get
4 The endless agenda had eight legal details added
5 Gale tested her stiff leg. He gnashed his big teeth.

Additional Drill

Think control as you key each line. If you make more than two errors on a line, repeat it. Keep your eyes on the copy in the text as you key

Key the following drill. Press ***Enter*** after each line.

1 His skin is thin; he is ill; he feels faint; see, he is ill.
2 He thinks it is a fad. I dislike that snide kid.
3 The kitten is a little lifeless and is an infant.

4 She shall indeed need that inside aid as enlisted.
5 His knife slid inside as the ill thief listened.
6 As the sled glides, the infant giggles in delight.

7 She disliked it. The kitten tangled that tinsel.
8 Tina, the gentle giant, giggled at Gina, the elf.
9 As she dashed ahead in glee, Leslie sang a jingle.
10 If he skis at night, Dad needs a light flashlight.

Introducing the Tab Key and Word Wrap

Tab Key

The first line of a paragraph is usually indented approximately one-half inch. In PKB, there is a preset tab every 0.5 inches.

Session 27

REINFORCEMENT: SESSIONS 1–26

Session Goals

Review keys from Sessions 1–26

10-Key Numeric Keypad: 25 WAM/0 errors
Alphabetic Keys: 30 WAM/2 errors

27.1-27.2 ON-SCREEN EXERCISES: GETTING STARTED

If you exited the program at the end of the previous session, refer to page 99 of Session 24 to review how to open the next session or to continue from where you left off.

27.3 TEXTBOOK EXERCISES: REINFORCEMENT

Earlier in the session you completed review drills presented on the screen. Now you will repeat some of those drills, along with some new ones, to reinforce your sense of where the alphabetic, number, and 10-key numeric keypad keys are located. When you have finished the drills, click Print (if desired), then click Next Exercise.

Alphabetic Sentences

Key lines 1–3 twice: first key the three lines for speed, then for control.

1 It seems that I missed the road; it makes me mad.
2 Those wrecked cars are in the ditch at the curve.
3 Endure the thousand, routine, suspended problems.

Top-Row Numbers

Key lines 1–9 twice: first key the nine lines for speed, then for control.

1 Find 5,000 medium weight legal size file folders.
2 The Merkel 9000 offers 23 channels with .6 watts.
3 Please trace orders 1169, 2978, 67890, and 14989.

4 Return the 420 reams of 16 lb. paper now, please.
5 She is purchasing a Group 4 857 Facsimile system.
6 I would like to have 9 shades and 16 gray scales.

To see how the preset tabs work, press the ***Tab*** key once, key the first word in the first column, press the ***Tab*** key twice, and key the first word in the second column. Press ***Enter*** to move to the next line of the first column. Repeat the process for the remaining lines.

→ lane → → Feat
→ tie → → Tease
→ aid → → That
→ nail → → Giant
→ leaf → → Fate

Word Wrap

When you key paragraphs of text (for example, in a letter), you do not need to press ***Enter*** at the end of each line. Word wrap is a feature that automatically wraps a word to the next line once that word exceeds the right margin. With word wrap, you need to press ***Enter*** only to end a paragraph, create a blank line, or end a short line (for example, a person's name in an envelope address).

Key the two paragraphs that follow. Use the ***Tab*** key to indent the first line of each paragraph and let word wrap move the insertion point to the next line. Press ***Enter*** twice at the end of each paragraph to leave a blank line between paragraphs.

→ An idle lad finishes last. He is shiftless as he sits and tells his tales. He needs an insight in the elegant things in life.

→ Allan is attaining a skill in legal defense. The giant task is thankless. He insists that all the details heighten his thinking.

Ending the Session

Now you may print this session's files, continue to the next session, or exit the program. See page 13 of Session 3 if you need to review procedures.

Ergonomic Tip

Don't choke the mouse; hold it lightly and click without using force.

- If you finish before time is up, start over.
- Press ***Tab*** with your "a" finger.
- Press ***Enter*** at the end of each line.

1	34	35	36	73	93	83	23	13	30	54	65	63
	345	636	663	663	663	336	393	393	993	93	339	936
	568	936	947	373	464	585	484	737	363	922	291	302
	3748	3833	9374	0585	0392	0458	0382	0483	3230	30339		
	4844	6673	8733	5663	5543	3323	6788	6733	2343	23343		

2	4844	6673	8733	5663	5543	3323	6788	6733	2343	23343		
	3748	3833	9374	0585	0392	0458	0382	0483	3230	30339		
	568	936	947	373	464	585	484	737	363	922	291	302
	345	636	663	663	663	336	393	393	993	993	339	936
	34	35	36	73	93	83	23	13	30	54	65	63

26.8 ONE-MINUTE TIMINGS

Goal: 30 WAM with no more than 2 errors

Take a 1-minute timing on each paragraph.

3 Students in school today must be prepared to live and compete in a global economy. They must develop a respect for life and work in a society of diverse cultures. Being exposed to the cultures of other countries can open doors to the future in terms of job opportunities.

4 The vessel sank in 510 feet of water in Lake Superior during a raging storm. An adept team of divers salvaged 149,683 parts. Seven local residents were among those who assisted in this job. The additional divers were welcome. The salvage company made a profit on their investment.

Ending the Session

Now you may print this session's files, continue to the next session, or exit the program. See page 103 of Session 24 if you need to review procedures.

Ergonomic Tip

Personalize your work area by having pictures of family and friends.

Session 6

REINFORCEMENT: SESSIONS 1–5

Session Goals

Review keys from Sessions 1–5

25 WAM/2 errors

6.1 On-Screen Exercises: Getting Started

If you are continuing immediately from Session 5, you are already warmed up and are looking at Exercise 6.2. Click the Next Exercise or Previous Exercise button if you are not at the correct exercise. The copy for Exercises 6.2 – 6.4 is in your text. Exercise 6.2 consists of two 1-minute timings.

If you exited the program at the end of the previous session, refer to page 11, Session 3 for instructions on entering the program.

6.2 CHECKING YOUR SKILL: ONE-MINUTE TIMINGS

The next activity in Session 6 is a timing to assess your keyboarding speed. You will see a message on the screen directing you to take two 1-minute timings on the paragraph that follows. If you finish the paragraph before time is up, strike ***Enter*** and start over. The program's "clock" begins when you strike the first key. When the time is up, the keyboard will "freeze," and the program calculates your words a minute (WAM) plus errors. Your goal is to key at least 25 words a minute (25 WAM) with no more than 2 errors. Be sure to use word wrap and indent the paragraph.

1 That gallant knight led the detail. A tall, thin lad assisted at the flank. The knight failed the task and feels the defeat. A sadness sifts in as his shield falls.

6.3 Textbook Exercises: Reinforcement

The Special Drills that follow provide additional practice on the keys that you have learned in Sessions 1–5. However, if you are already keying over 25 WAM with no more than 2 errors and do not hesitate when keying, Click the Next Exercise button three times. This will take you to Session 7, Exercise 2.

If you are not at the 25 WAM level, and/or are making more than 2 errors, proceed with the Special Drills to build speed and/or accuracy. Here are guidelines for choosing drills:

1. If you have not mastered a key reach (you hesitate before striking the key), key the speed-building lines.
2. If you are not keying at least 25 WAM, key the speed-building lines.
3. If you are making more than 2 errors per minute, key the accuracy-building lines. If you make more than two errors on a line, key it again.

2 Drill

Key lines 1–5 twice: first key the five lines for speed, then for control. Read the numbers in groups.

1 52 52 52 52 52 52 25 25 25 25 25 24 24 42 62 72 82 52
2 25 62 72 82 92 02 42 52 27 85 58 85 95 96 90 88 56 24
3 242 252 252 262 852 258 158 148 284 282 272 958 594

4 222 224 225 226 227 228 228 822 922 202 202 212 2169
5 2456 2789 2010 2456 2678 2525 24567 27890 12456 127

3 Drill

Key lines 1–5 twice: first key the five lines for speed, then for control. Read the numbers in groups.

1 63 63 63 63 63 36 36 36 36 36 93 39 39 39 69 69 63 34 35
2 36 73 73 93 83 23 13 30 54 65 63 36 83 49 34 234 354 345
3 456 383 838 938 736 373 369 936 963 33 568 936 947 373

4 464 585 484 737 363 922 291 302 30 4435 4344 3345 3443
5 2343 2334 4873 4848 3929 26282 4844 6673 8733 5663 55

Additional Drill

At the end of each line proofread. If you have any errors, repeat the line until you can key it without error before going to the next line.

Key the following drill for control. Press ***Enter*** after each line.

1 41 41 51 61 71 81 91 11 141 141 141 141 145 146 14
2 100 104 145 414 151 149 109 011 084 171 155 109 1
3 4111 1444 4568 1787 1679 88981 98871 019091 001001

4 24 56 25 58 47 71 89 80 20 20 20 50 50 20 70 45 86
5 456 789 125 125 128 124 126 129 125 128 982 982 12
6 2222 2525 2582 2582 9792 2728 26267 88771 07862 72

7 345 636 663 663 663 336 393 393 993 993 339 936 93
8 568 936 947 373 464 585 484 737 363 922 291 302 30
9 4844 6673 8733 5663 5543 3323 6788 6733 2343 23343

26.7 TIMINGS: 10-KEY NUMERIC KEYPAD

Goal: 25 WAM with 0 errors

- Take a 1-minute timing on the lines in Group 1. Then take two 1-minute timings on the lines in Group 2.

Once you have completed the drills, click Print (if desired), then click the Next Exercise button. The program will then direct you to take two more 1-minute timings.

Special Drills

- Key each line once.
- If you need more practice, key the group of lines again.

Balanced-Hand Words (Speed)

1 and the ant sit ale elf end hen she end sigh sign
2 aid fit sit did tie die dig fig and the hang then
3 halt than hand lens lake lane then than sign fish

4 idle lens lane sigh then dish disk sign half lake
5 shake snake title aisle angle fight handle island
6 angle sight digit gland eight slant height sleigh
7 signal giant tight an he if it and elf the and he

Letter Combinations (Speed)

1 de den dead deal desk denial dense deft dental
2 di dig dish dial digest dislike dine dike disk
3 I dislike the heat dial that fits the dental fan.

4 fi fish final fine finish fight find fig field finale
5 ga gal gas gag gale gait gallant gasket gadget
6 Gal, finished the gasket and the gas gadget gate.

7 ha hate halt half hash hang handle hand hat had
8 ki kite kindle kilt kiln king kink kit kind
9 That hanging kite tail has halted the hail.

10 le lest left lead lend ledge least leaf lean lease
11 li lid lie lied lien link linking linkage like
12 At least link the left lid and let the length stand.

13 sa sad sat safe sake sale said sang Sal saline
14 si sit site sitting signal sighted sill silken sip siding
15 Sad Sal sang a signal as she sighted a safe site.

Session 26 1, 2, 3

Session Goals

1, 2, 3

10-Key Numeric Keypad: 25 WAM/0 errors
Alphabetic Keys: 30 WAM/2 errors

26.1-26.5 On-Screen Exercises: Getting Started

If you exited the program at the end of the previous session, refer to page 99 of Session 24 to review how to open the next session or to continue from where you left off.

26.6 Textbook Exercises: Reinforcement

Earlier in the session you completed new-key drills presented on the screen. Now you will repeat some of those drills, along with some new ones, to reinforce your keyboarding skills. When you have finished the drills, click Print (if desired), then Next Exercise.

Reviewing the 1, 2, and 3 Keys

1 Drill

Key lines 1–5 twice: first key the five lines for speed, then for control. Read the numbers in groups and press ***Enter*** at the end of each line.

1 41 14 41 41 41 14 14 14 451 415 514 614 614 716 41
2 61 61 61 51 71 81 91 17 171 171 187 187 191 151 19
3 168 187 187 186 175 177 109 186 101 186 186 19658

4 145 156 195 157 145 198 966 919 818 717 616 515 41
5 1474 4010 4561 4561 4710 46678 15851 979711 5987

16 st stead steal steadiness stateside stag state
17 ta tag talk take tale taste task tan tap tape tail
18 Steadfast star stands and talks and then sits.

19 Te tea test tenth tend tenant tease teak tent
20 th then that than thing this theft thin thesis
21 Then that tested tenant, Ted, did a tenth tea test.

Double-Letter Words (Accuracy)

1 see glee needs indeed feeling needless teens seed
2 egg sell sniff haggle falling eggshell stall eggs
3 eel keen sheen needle fiddles seedling sleek deed

4 add kiss stiff assist endless lifeless still hill
5 fee need sheet seeing dissent likeness steed heel
6 add fell skill allied skilled settling shell tell

7 see feel teeth indeed gallant sledding sleet knee
8 all hall shall little install knitting stall tall
9 Sadness is a feeling I assess as an alleged need.

10 Assist the skiing attendant and lessen all falls.
11 The sleek kitten shall flee the illegal attendants.
12 Haggling is a senseless dissent that is needless.
13 Flatten the stiff fiddle and install the tassels.

Longer Words (Accuracy)

1 endless athlete flatten inflated install disliked
2 lenient distant delighted heading inkling digital
3 A lenient athlete has inflated the flattened keg.

4 Hesitating likeness indefinite alkaline initiated
5 heightened stealing gaslight lengthened delegates
6 The hesitating delegate is stealing the gaslight.

7 Landslide skinflint stateside essential legislate
8 negligent lightness sightless delighted attendant
9 tasteless steadfast defendant thankless seashells
10 Seashells in the landslide delighted a skinflint.

9 9678 9687 8985 9678 96745 45678 56789 98765 987654

25.7 TIMINGS: 10-KEY NUMERIC KEYPAD

Goal: 25 WAM with 0 errors

- Take a 1-minute timing on the lines in Group 1. Then take two 1-minute timings on the lines in Group 2.
- If you finish before time is up, start over.
- Press ***Tab*** with your "a" finger.
- Press ***Enter*** at the end of each line.

1	99	89	89	79	79	66	69	69	59	59	49	49
	789	789	456	456	475	678	789	908	970	970	987	09
	900	909	909	969	696	898	797	690	578	589	987	95
	9678	9687	8985	6978	96745	45678	56789	98765	987654			
	9889	8899	9999	7999	69969	69969	94569	49566	594695			

2	9889	8899	9999	7999	69969	69969	94569	49566	594695			
	9678	9687	8985	6978	96745	45678	56789	98765	987654			
	900	909	909	969	969	696	898	797	690	578	589	987
	789	789	456	456	475	678	789	908	970	970	987	09
	99	89	89	79	79	66	69	69	59	59	49	49

25.8 ONE-MINUTE TIMINGS

Goal: 30 WAM with no more than 2 errors

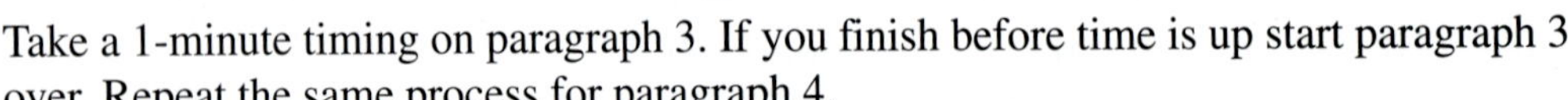

Take a 1-minute timing on paragraph 3. If you finish before time is up start paragraph 3 over. Repeat the same process for paragraph 4.

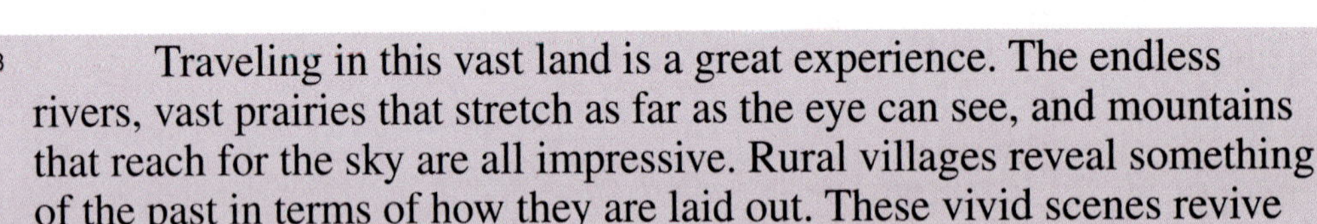

3 Traveling in this vast land is a great experience. The endless rivers, vast prairies that stretch as far as the eye can see, and mountains that reach for the sky are all impressive. Rural villages reveal something of the past in terms of how they are laid out. These vivid scenes revive the mind and lift the spirits.

4 During your working life, you will meet and work with people of many different cultures. Although each of us is a member of a racial or ethnic group, our work groups make up one large community. The beliefs we share give us a common base and a list of topics to discuss.

ENDING THE SESSION

Now you may print this session's files, continue to the next session, or exit the program. See page 103 of Session 24 if you need to review procedures.

Ergonomic Tip

For relaxation, lightly clench hand and release, fanning out fingers, five times.

6.4 ONE-MINUTE TIMINGS

Now that you have completed the drills, take two 1-minute timings on the following paragraph. Compare the rates with your first attempts. Has your speed improved? Do you have fewer errors? If you are not reaching 25 WAM with 2 or fewer errors, repeat Sessions 1–5.

1 That gallant knight led the detail. A tall, thin lad assisted at the flank. The knight failed the task and feels the defeat. A sadness sifts in as his shield falls.

Ending the Session

At the end of each session, you have three options:

- Print any documents you have created.
- Continue with the next session.
- Exit Snap Paradigm Keyboarding.

Print

To print Exercises 6.1 and 6.3, follow the directions found on page 14.

To print the timed writings for this session (Exercises 6.2 and 6.4), take the following steps:

1. Click the Close button in the top right corner of the screen.
2. At your Paradigm Keyboarding with Snap Welcome page, point to Reports on the Snap menu bar, and click View Submissions Report.
3. At the View Submissions Report Wizard, click Show timings files to see the timings text (Exercises 6.2 and 6.4).
4. Click Show Report.
5. Click 006tim.
6. At the Word Processor dialog box, click Launch.
7. Click File, and then click Print.
8. At the Print dialog box, click OK.
9. Click the Close button to close the Paradigm Word Processor.
10. Click Home on the Snap menu bar to return to the Welcome page.

Continue

To continue on the next session, click the Next Exercise button **twice**. This will take you to Exercise 7.2. (You will bypass Exercise 7.1 Warmup since you are already warmed up.)

Exit

To exit, do the following:

1. Click the Close button in the top right corner of the screen.
2. At your Paradigm Keyboarding with Snap Welcome page, click Logout.

Ergonomic Tip

Keep your mouse at the same height and distance as your keyboard.

3 67 67 67 67 67 67 76 76 76 76 67 76 76 76 67 6 777

4 76 74 74 567 567 567 567 567 4567 4567 7 456 457
5 65 45 67 4567 6 777 765 7567 5560 57670 5666 056
6 70 45670 45670 567 5560 5456 6747 44760 547 645

8 Drill

Key lines 1–5 twice: first key the five lines for speed, then for control. Read the numbers as groups.

1 555 58 58 58 58 58 58 58 58 85 85 85 85 85 85 58 5
2 58 68 68 68 48 48 48 48 58 78 78 78 78 58 58 6 800 8
3 800 800 807 807 806 805 508 508 408 804 88 876 568

4 468 780 786 807 876 558 558 558 778 78 45678 87654
5 007 80765 876 8888 7787 7877 6778 5678 458 85 8685

9 Drill

Key lines 1–5 twice: first key the five lines for speed, then for control. Think of the numbers in groups.

1 69 69 69 69 99 99 99 66 66 66 69 69 69 69 69 66 66 990
2 90 90 90 98 98 98 97 79 79 89 89 69 69 96 96 96 789 78
3 9 456 456 475 678 789 908 908 970 970 987 09 890 890

4 690 906 960 978 589 479 690 978 890 89 6989 6989 697
5 9 6979 69879 69879 69857 96857 456789 9678 9687 898

Additional Drill

Key the following drill for control. Press ***Enter*** after each line.

1 456 45 67 67 65 64 675 456 456 456 456 4567 4567 67
2 765 657 654 475 476 457 45776 4576 45577 45567 467
3 576 475 777 777 667 666 65777 7445 57774 77745 774

4 876 568 678 468 780 786 807 876 558 558 558 778 788
5 45678 87654 80765 876 8888 7787 7877 6778 5678 458
6 80000 87778 88585 848 5858 8585 5857 5857 8575 885

7 789 789 456 456 475 678 789 908 908 970 970 987 09 9
8 900 909 909 969 969 696 898 797 690 578 589 987 95 9

At the end of each line, proofread. If you have any errors, repeat the line until you can key it without error before going to the next liine.

Session 7: P, R, QUESTION MARK

Session Goals

P, R, and Question Mark

-ed and -ing word endings

25 WAM/2 errors

7.1–7.7 On-Screen Exercises: Getting Started

If you exited the program at the end of the previous session, refer to page 11 of Session 3 to review how to open the next session or to continue from where you left off.

7.8 Textbook Exercises: Reinforcement

Some of the drills presented earlier in Session 7 are repeated here, along with some new drills, to give you Reinforcement practice. After completing the Reinforcement activities, click the Print button (if desired), then click the Next Exercise button.

Reviewing the P, R, and Question Mark Keys

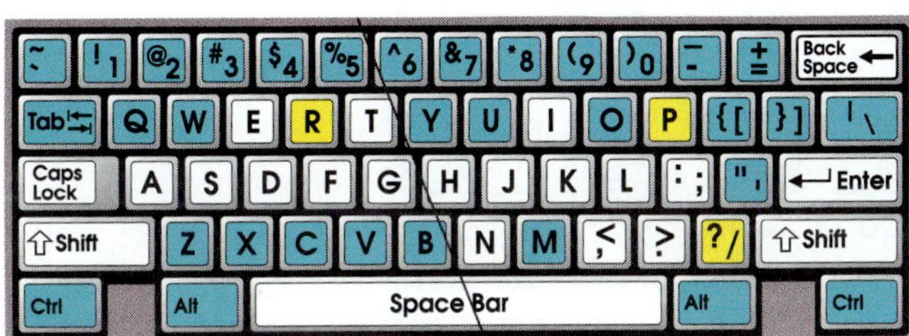

R Key

P Key

Question Mark Key

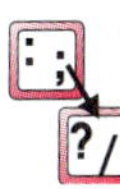

P Drill

Key lines 1–3 once, pushing for speed.

1 ;p pan pat pea peg pen pep pet pie pig pin pit pails
2 ;p ship tape pink skip slap taps gaps pest sap paste
3 Peasant Pennant Pitfall Patient Pheasant Pleasant Philadelphia

Session 25 7, 8, 9

Session Goals

7, 8, 9

10-Key Numeric Keypad: 25 WAM/0 errors
Alphabetic Keys: 30 WAM/2 errors

25.1-25.5 On-Screen Exercises: Getting Started

If you exited the program at the end of the previous session, refer to page 99 of Session 24 to review how to open the next session or to continue from where you left off.

25.6 Textbook Exercises: Reinforcement

Some of the drills presented on the screen earlier in the session are repeated in the text, along with some new ones, to reinforce your sense of where the keys are located on the numeric keypad. When you have finished the drills, click Print (if desired), then Next Exercise.

Reviewing the 7, 8, and 9 Keys

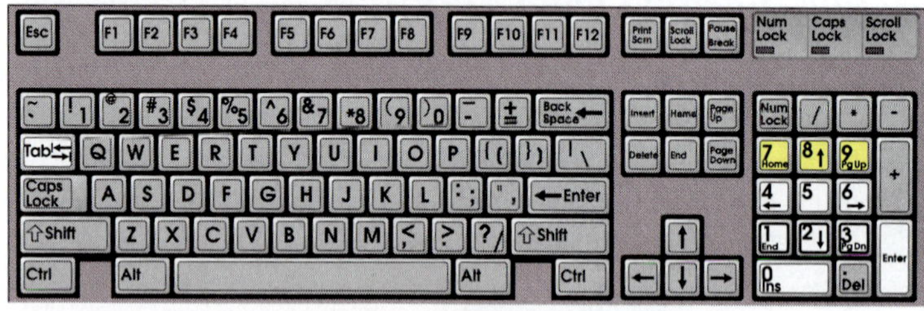

Drill Instructions

- Use your "a" finger to tap the ***Tab*** key.
- Press ***Enter*** at the end of each line.

7 Drill

Key lines 1–6 twice: first key the six lines for speed, then for control. Remember to read the numbers as groups.

1 444 47 47 47 47 47 47 47 74 74 74 74 74 74 74 74 4
2 57 57 57 57 57 57 57 75 75 75 75 75 75 75 75 5 666

Key lines 4–6 once, focusing on either speed or control. If you are focusing on control and you make more than two errors on a line, repeat it.

4 A tall, split, peeling aspen sapling is diseased.
5 Pat speaks and pleads and defends the plaintiffs.
6 Did Jane tape that splint and dispense the pills?

R Drill

Key lines 1–3 twice: first key line 1 for speed, then key line 1 for control. If you make more than 2 errors on line 1 when keying for control, repeat it. Follow the same procedure for lines 2 and 3.

1 fr rain rare real rink rake rage rear ripe rip rage rigid
2 stare there their after pride tired far her press jar tear
3 Refrain Repress Release Retreat Resident Register Reap

Question Mark Drill

Important: Tap the space bar **once** after the question mark at the end of the sentence. This rule applies to all end-of-sentence punctuation when you are using a proportional font such as Times New Roman. When a question mark ends a line in the drill, press ***Enter*** immediately—do not tap the space bar.

Key lines 1–3 once, keeping your eyes on the copy.

1 Is Jennie ahead? Is Dennis safe? Is Allen late?
2 Is Ken late? Is Dale fit? Is Neil in his teens?
3 Did she dine? Did the leaf fall? Did Jane flee?

Additional Drill

Key the following drill. Press ***Enter*** after each line.

1 In the sleet, a sheep passed the pines and plants.
2 In his pastel sedan, Jake passed that fast jeep.
3 His left thigh is gashed; the patient is in pain.

4 rest tree trip hire ring fire earn hard dirt fair
5 range ridge raise reign rinse art jar rinse right
6 eager fir ran after heart large dress greed green

7 Shall I still slide in the infield if Jake faints?
8 Has she hit? Has the thief left? Has he landed?
9 Is Dale fit? Is Neil in his teens? Is Ken late?

Think control as you key each line. If you make more than two errors on a line, repeat it. Keep your eyes on the copy in the text as you key.

3 Current periodicals and programs are promoting the need for international business education courses. Another trend is to include international concepts in existing courses and programs. The global view of business and international protocols must be taught to students preparing for the world of work.

4 Basically, employers like a loyal employee. Honesty and courtesy always pay off in any job or assignment. Apathy and sloppy work are always very costly to a company. On the other hand, any employee who does consistently good work will be properly awarded and can expect to receive a salary increase of perhaps 8 percent.

Ending the Session

Now you may print this session's files, continue to the next session, or exit the program.

Print

To print Exercises 24.1 – 24.6 proceed as follows:

1 Click the Close button in the top right corner of the screen.
2 At your Paradigm Keyboarding with Snap Welcome page, point to Reports on the Snap menu bar, and click View Submissions Report.
3 At the View Submissions Report Wizard, click Show session files to see the drill lines text (Exercises 24.1-24.4), or Show timings files to see the timings text (Exercises 24.5-24.6).
4 Click Show Report.
5 Click the name of the file you want to print.
6 At the Word Processor dialog box, click Launch.
7 Click File, and then click Print.
8 At the Print dialog box, click OK.
9 Click the Close button to close the Paradigm Word Processor.
10 Click Home on the Snap menu bar to return to the Welcome page.

Continue

To continue on the next session, click the Next Exercise button **twice**. This will take you to Exercise 25.2. (You will bypass Exercise 25.1 Warmup since you are already warmed up.)

Exit

To exit, do the following:

1 Click the Close button in the top right corner of the screen.
2 At your Paradigm Keyboarding with Snap Welcome page, click Logout.

Ergonomic Tip

Keep neck and shoulders relaxed.

What Is a Keyboarding Error?

Some errors affect only the appearance of a document. On the other hand, certain keyboarding errors can have a drastic effect on the message being communicated. Consider the result of transposing two numbers in a customer's invoice; for example, keying $19 instead of $91. Following is a list of some common keyboarding mistakes. You will find reviewing the list helpful to ensure that you are aware of possible errors as you complete timings and later as you prepare letters and other documents.

Common Keyboarding Errors

- Keying wrong words
- Transposing numbers
- Placing extra spaces between words or numbers
- Placing a space before a punctuation mark
- Not capitalizing a proper noun or the first word of a sentence
- Capitalizing a word in a sentence that should not be capitalized
- Placing too many spaces after a punctuation mark or between paragraphs
- Using improper left, right, top, or bottom margins
- Not indenting properly
- Being inconsistent in vertical spacing
- Using incorrect punctuation

Checking Your Skill

In Session 6 you completed a 1-minute timing. The goals for the timing under the Timings Check that follows are based on your performance in Session 6. If you don't remember your scores, you can review them by accessing the Timings Performance Report from your Paradigm Keyboarding Snap home page, as explained below.

Viewing the Report

You can check your timings scores in the Timings Performance Report by taking the following steps:

1. Exit your current session.
2. Go to your Paradigm Keyboarding with Snap Welcome page.
3. Point to Reports and click Timings Performance Report.
4. At the Timings Performance Report wizard, click Show Report.
5. A table appears showing each timing you have attempted, along with your WAM and number of errors.
6. Click the Show Graph button to see this information in graph form.
7. To return to a keyboarding session, click Home on your Snap menu bar, and then click the name of the next exercise you wish to do.

1 654 654 456 456 456 456 456 655 556 556 664 664 56
2 456 546 546 546 645 456 546 566 566 664 665 444 44
3 544 544 566 544 644 644 554 555 444 655 444 555 44

4 64 456 456 654 456 666 444 555 654 654 456 456 456
5 45 666 555 444 654 654 465 55 44 45 65 64 56 54 446
6 500 600 400 545 545 6545 4505 5460 5440 5540 50404

7 644 654 4560 4560 4560 4560 6540 6540 6540 450 406
8 556 654 6540 5460 5046 0564 0546 5040 5000 605 404
9 600 500 4000 4005 5004 6005 5004 6005 0665 044 606

24.5 TIMINGS: 10-KEY NUMERIC KEYPAD

Goal: 25 WAM with 0 errors

- Take a 1-minute timing on the lines in Group 1. Then take two 1-minute timings on the lines in Group 2.
- If you finish before time is up, start over.
- Press the *Tab* key with your "a" finger.
- Press *Enter* at the end of each line.

1	654	654	654	456	456	666	444	555	546	546	546	456	46
	555	666	444	555	654	555	456	456	654	645	645	645	45
	654	654	456	456	456	456	456	655	556	556	664	664	56
	456	546	546	546	645	456	546	566	566	644	665	444	44
	544	544	566	544	644	644	554	555	444	655	444	555	44

2	550	600	540	540	650	6540	6440	4560	6540	6054	56605
	500	600	400	545	545	6545	4505	5460	5440	5540	50404
	644	654	4560	4560	4560	4560	6540	6540	6540	450	406
	556	654	6540	5460	5046	0564	0546	5040	5000	605	404
	600	500	4000	4005	5004	6005	5004	6005	0665	044	606

24.6 ONE-MINUTE TIMINGS

Goal: 30 WAM with no more than 2 errors

- Take a 1-minute timing on paragraph 3, then take a 1-minute timing on paragraph 4.
- Press *Tab* to indent the first line.
- If you finish a paragraph before time is up, start over.

7.9 ONE-MINUTE TIMINGS

Take a 1-minute timing on each paragraph; if you finish before time is up, start over. If you did not reach at least 25 WAM on your most recent timing, push for speed. If you are keying at least 25 WAM but are making more than 2 errors per minute, concentrate on accuracy. If you are above 25 WAM and are making 2 or fewer errors, push for speed.

1 Jane prepares legal papers and letters. She prefers reading ledgers and graphs. It is tiring and drains her. If she falters at the start, Jane is risking a defeat. The stern leader sees her stress and praises her spirit.

2 Print the paragraph in large letters. Raise the title and delete the digraphs. Insert three fresh phrases at the end. It is all right if Dane deletes that first phrase. It is a danger and a threat. Perhaps the ending is right.

ENDING THE SESSION

Now you may print this session's files, continue to the next session, or exit the program. See page 24 of Session 6 if you need to review procedures.

Ergonomic Tip

Your hands are to float or glide above the keyboard, not rest.

Drill Instructions

- Use the "a" finger of your left hand on the ***Tab*** key to space between groups of numbers. Anchor your "F" finger when making the reach to the Tab key.
- Press ***Enter*** at the end of each line.
- Keep your eyes on the copy.
- Read the numbers as combinations (review page 53 if necessary).

Note: If you want your numbers to appear in a single column rather than as a line, press ***Enter*** after keying each group of numbers. However, creating a single column requires extra paper when printing.

Home Row Drill

Place your right hand on home row (4, 5, 6). Use your right little finger for ***Enter***, **plus,** and **minus.** Use your "a" finger to depress the ***Tab*** key.

Key lines 1–5 twice: first key the five lines for speed, then for control. Remember to think of the numbers in groups. Assume that you are in a spreadsheet application; tab after keying each group of numbers. Press ***Enter*** at the end of each line.

1 456 456 456 456 456 456 456 456 456 456 456 456 45
2 456 456 456 654 654 564 564 654 564 565 564 456 46
3 456 456 456 654 654 555 444 666 456 654 456 456 64

4 654 654 654 456 456 666 444 555 546 546 546 456 46
5 555 666 444 555 654 555 456 456 654 645 645 645 45

Students in Online Classes

If you look at your fingers or the screen as you are entering the numbers, it will slow you down. Also, when keying the lines for control, stop at the end of each line and proofread. If you have three or more errors, repeat the line.

0 Drill

Place the thumb of your right hand on the 0 key, your "a" finger on the ***Tab*** key. Tab after each group of numbers. Press **Enter** after each line.

Key lines 1–5 twice: first key the five lines for speed, then for control.

1 0 00 000 000 000 000 50 50 50 50 50 50 60 60 40 400
2 400 400 400 400 500 500 600 600 500 400 400 500 60
3 405 504 506 605 440 400 550 660 660 550 440 456 60

4 440 500 450 450 560 4560 4560 4560 6540 6540 56000
5 550 600 540 540 650 6540 6440 4560 6540 6054 56605

Students in Online Classes

After keying each line for control, proofread. If you have any errors, repeat the line until you can key it without error.

Additional Drill

Key the following drill for control. Press ***Enter*** after each line.

8.1- 8.8 **ON-SCREEN EXERCISES: GETTING STARTED**

If you exited the program at the end of the previous session, refer to page 11 of Session 3 to review how to open the next session or to continue from where you left off.

8.9 **TEXTBOOK EXERCISES: REINFORCEMENT**

Some of the drills you completed during the first portion of Session 8 are presented here, along with some new drills, to reinforce your skills with the new key reaches. When you are finished keying the drills, click Print (if desired), then click Next Exercise.

Reviewing the M and V Keys

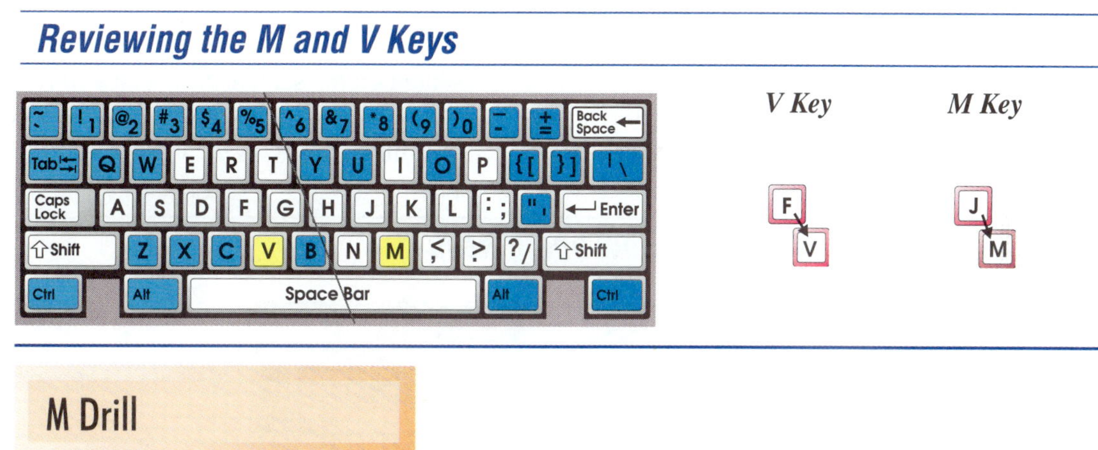

M Drill

Key lines 1–3 once, pushing for speed.

1 jm am am him him man man mad mad jam jam me me mean
2 might might metal metal dream dream ram ram made made
3 Mashed Mean Mailed Minted Melted Makes Melt Might Mild

The following illustration shows the general arrangement of most 10-key numeric keypads. The top row of numbers contains the 7, 8, and 9. The middle row contains the 4, 5, and 6. This row is identified as the *home row*. The bottom row of keys contains the 1, 2, and 3. The ***0*** (zero) key is at the very bottom. When working with spreadsheets, the ***Tab*** key ("a" finger) is used to move across the screen from cell to cell. The ***Enter*** key is a larger key located to the right of the ***3*** key. It is used to move vertically from one line to the next.

On a microcomputer the Num Lock key must be "on" to use the 10-key numeric keypad. When Num Lock is on, a green light displays by Num Lock in the upper-right corner of the keyboard. If Num Lock is not on, press ***Num Lock*** to turn it on. Press again to turn it off.

Alternate 10-Key Numeric Keypad Configurations

In addition to the standard numeric keypad configuration, there are several alternate key arrangements used among computer manufacturers. Typically, the symbol keys (***plus [+]***, ***minus [-]***, ***Enter***, and ***decimal***) are rearranged. Other keys often rearranged include diagonal/forward slash (/) and asterisk (*). Generally, using the symbol keys next to the 10-key pad is more efficient.

Study the configuration of your 10-key pad and become familiar with the arrangement of the keys. Then proceed with the on-screen activities.

24.4 Textbook Exercises: Reinforcement

Earlier in the session you completed new-key drills presented on the screen. Now you will repeat some of those drills and key some new ones to reinforce your sense of where the keys are on the 10-key numeric keypad. When you have finished the drills, click Print (if desired), then click Next Exercise.

Reviewing the Home Row and 0 Keys

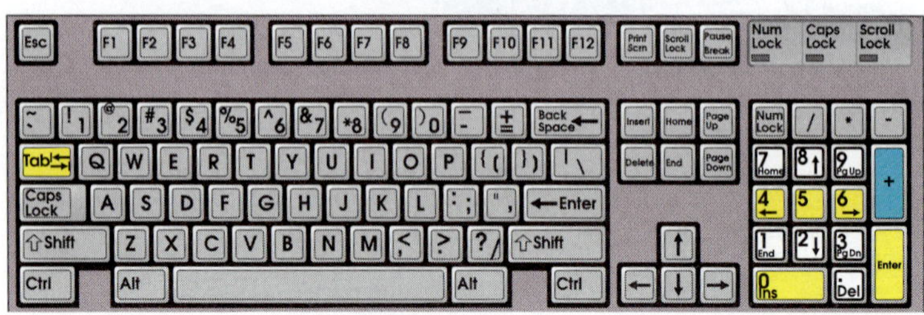

Key lines 4–6 twice, concentrating on control.

4 Mike is making a frame; he needs ample sandpaper.
5 Did Mamie transmit the message after amending it?
6 Did Sammie eliminate all mistakes in the message?

V Drill

Key lines 1–3 once, focusing on speed.

1 fv dive dive five five give give grieve grieve drive
2 private private deliver deliver veteran even even vein
3 Negative Negative Seven Seven Advertising Advertising

Key lines 4–6 twice; concentrate on control.

4 Did Van ever deliver the varnish and the shelves?
5 It is evident; the vital lever reverses the vent at five.
6 Marvia served vanilla malts at the private event in Vail.

Additional Drill

Key the following drill. Press ***Enter*** after each line.

1 The malt that Pam made had milk and mint in it.
2 The fine farm animal, Sandman, had a marked limp.
3 Mail the letter at midnight and add ample stamps.

4 Is that smashed metal mass a damaged helmet, Jim?
5 As her mind dimmed, Minne missed the main message.
6 In a lavish, private plane, the traveler arrived.

7 At the evening event, seven silver vases vanished.
8 Give him a vitamin, the driver has a grave fever.
9 Five vigilant servants evaded the starved vandal.
10 Did Val deliver that vast velvet divan this evening?

Students in Online Classes

Key lines 1–3 for speed; key lines 4–6 for control, repeat the lines if you have more than two errors; key lines 7–10 for speed. Remember to keep your eyes on the text as you key.

8.10 ONE-MINUTE TIMINGS

Goal: 25 WAM with no more than 2 errors

- Take a 1-minute timing on each paragraph.
- If you finish a paragraph before time is up, start over.

Session 24 HOME ROW (4, 5, 6), 0

Session Goals

Home Row (4, 5, 6), 0

10-Key Numeric Keypad: 25 WAM/0 errors
Alphabetic Keys: 30 WAM/2 errors

24.1-24.3 ON-SCREEN EXERCISES: GETTING STARTED

If you are continuing immediately from Session 23, begin with Exercise 24.1. Click the Next Exercise or Previous Exercise button if you are not at the correct exercise.

If you exited the program at the end of the previous session, refer to page 11, Session 3 for instructions on entering the program.

Before beginning the on-screen activities for Exercise 24.1, read the text on pages 99 and 100 titled "Typical 10-Key Numeric Keypad Configuration" and "Alternate 10-Key Numeric Keypad Configurations."

TYPICAL 10-KEY NUMERIC KEYPAD CONFIGURATION

Microcomputers have a 10-key numeric keypad located to the right of the alphabetic keyboard. The numeric keypad allows you to enter numeric data with one hand. This keypad may be used instead of the numeric row on the alphabetic keyboard. One example of using the 10-key numeric keypad is in working with spreadsheets and entering numbers in cells and rows. With a minimum amount of practice, you can enter numeric data at speeds well over 100 digits per minute. By industry standards, a rate of 250 digits per minute is considered average (equivalent to 50 WAM).

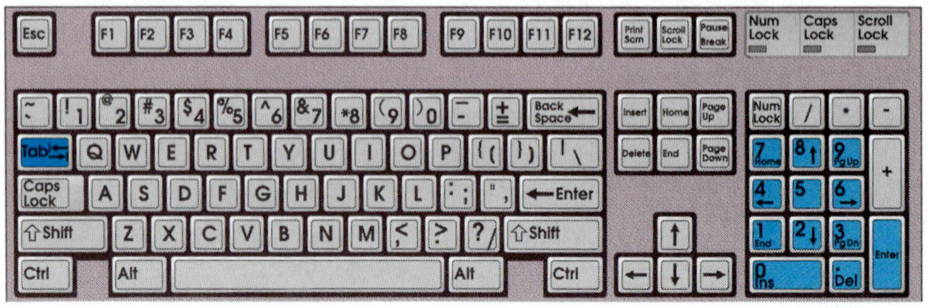

1 Marna smelled the simmering meat. The steam permeated the air. She managed a small taste and smiled. The meat and milk might help that little girl and ease her pain.

2 As he firmed the damp earth at the tree, the miser imagined he heard a small sigh. Mirages in the misted marsh alarmed him. Grim fears emerged as his mindless tramping faltered.

3 Make that simple diagram first. Then send a message in the mail. Tell that salesman that his latest remarks made the manager mad. The meeting impaired the imminent merger.

4 Traveling in this vast native land is a near marvel. The savage rivers and varied paved miles are impressive. Vivid sights revive the mind and lift spirits. Villages reveal veiled vestiges; a dividend is derived.

5 Even if Gavin is vain, she has avid fans and attentive friends. Her singing is sensitive; she reveals her vast talent. She deserves lavish and vivid praise. Her versatile verses are a massive advantage and elevate her fevered fans.

6 Navigate the even trail in life. Derive all things that are pleasant and reap the advantages. Preserve the vital past and evade vile evils. An avid, aggressive striving is needed in all lives. A varied and diverse path prevents grief.

Ending the Session

Now you may print this session's files, continue to the next session, or exit the program. See page 24 of Session 6 if you need to review procedures.

Ergonomic Tip

Position your monitor so that the top of the screen is no higher than your eye level.

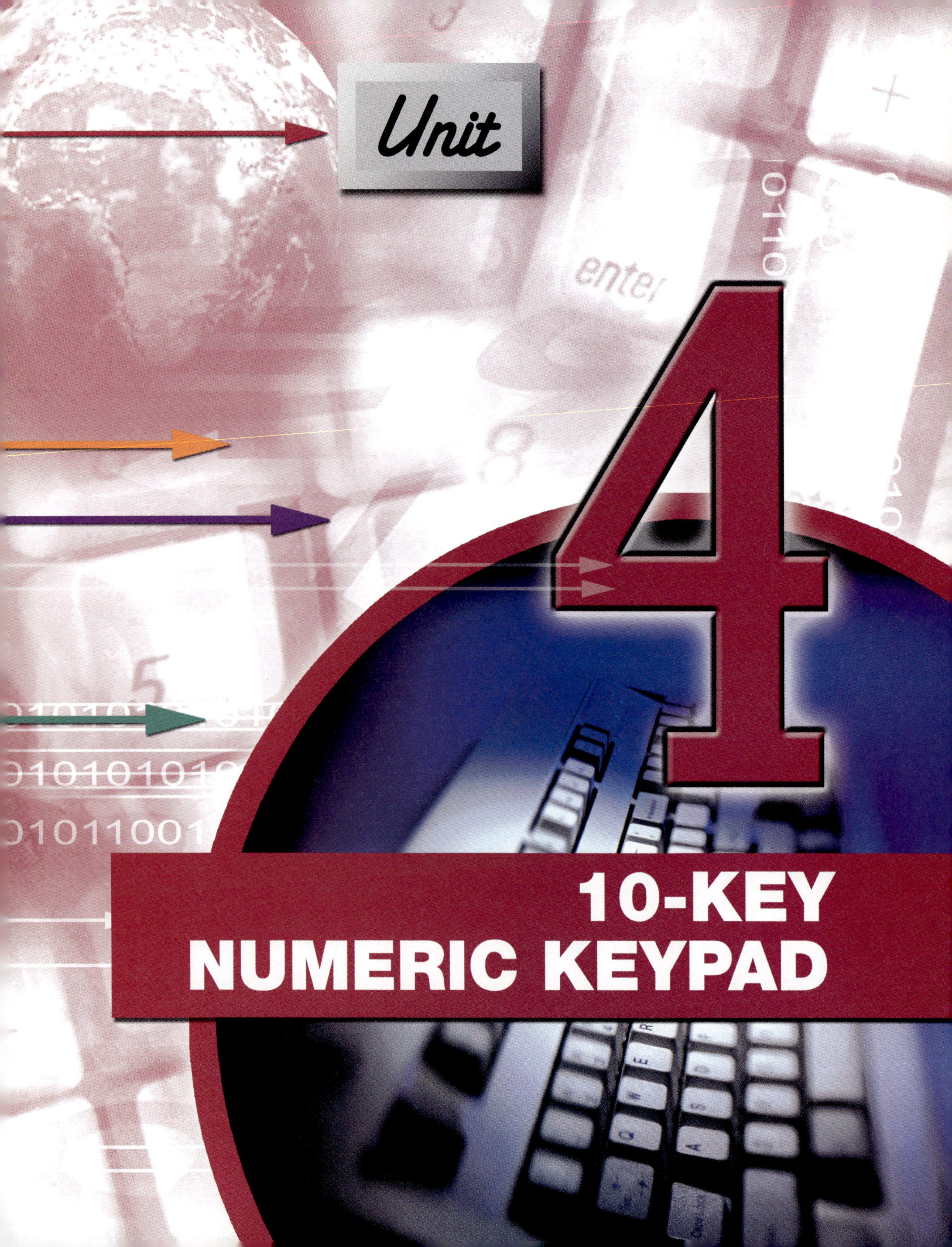
Unit
4
10-KEY
NUMERIC KEYPAD

Session 9: O, B, W

9.1-9.10 On-Screen Exercises: Getting Started

If you exited the program at the end of the previous session, refer to page 11 of Session 3 to review how to open the next session or to continue from where you left off.

9.11 Textbook Exercises: Reinforcement

Some of the drills you completed during the first portion of Session 9 are repeated here, along with some new ones, to reinforce your learning of the O, B, and W keys. A Thinking Drill exercise then follows. When you have finished these exercises, click Print (if desired), then click Next Exercise.

Reviewing the O, B, and W Keys

W Key *B Key* *O Key*

O Drill

Key lines 1–3, pushing for speed.

1 lo do for hop log one old not off pot son golf long
2 along avoid drove prior other toast option oppose some
3 Endorse Diamond Another Visitor Develop Insertion Potato

2 Malaysia is in the process of shifting from an agricultural to an industrial economy. Their government has a plan entitled Vision 2020 that will make them fully industrialized by that year. Many government and business people feel that the ethnic balance of Malay, Chinese, and Indian races must remain intact. Banks are offering low-interest loans for Malay-owned businesses.

3 A lazy bicycle ride in the country is surely a healthy and worthy activity. A sunny sky and a dry day is surely an omen to any type of cyclist. Be wary of cloudy and windy days. A daily remedy for a healthy and spry body is a ride on a cycle. Energy is enjoyed by young and not so young.

23.10 THREE–MINUTE TIMINGS

Goal: 25 WAM/2 errors

Take two 3-minute timings on the following paragraph.

1 Newer houses seem to cost more and have more space in them. Homes are built with large master bedrooms and have such things as walk-in closets, double sinks, and sitting space. Most homes also have two major rooms: a formal living room and a large family room. Houses that used to sell for reasonable amounts are now priced in the hundreds of thousands of dollars. In parts of the country people pay over $250,000 for a new, average-sized house.

ENDING THE SESSION

Now you may print this session's files, continue to the next session, or exit the program. See page 75 of Session 18 if you need to review procedures.

Ergonomic Tip

Use your entire hand to depress hard-to-reach keys rather than forcing hands into awkward positions. Make sure that you bring your fingers back to the home row keys.

Key lines 4–6 once for control. If you make more than two errors on a line, repeat it.

4 Ora ordered the onions and olives from the store.
5 The soft fog floated aloft over the lone trooper.
6 Did the florist remove the thorns from the roses?

B Drill

Key lines 1–3 once; push for speed.

1 fb bad bag ban bar bat bed beg Ben bet bid big bit
2 barter member harbor banker ballot border benefit brake
3 Alphabet Basement Neighbor Remember Remarkable Be

Key lines 4–6 twice: Key line 4 for speed, then key line 4 for control. Follow the same procedure for lines 5 and 6.

4 I grabbed a dab of bread and biked to the harbor.
5 Babe is baffled; the beverage bottles are broken.
6 Barni, the beagle, barks and begs for a big bone.

W Drill

Key lines 1–3 once, pushing for speed.

1 sw jaw wag raw two war wet saw hew how new sew snow
2 review warmer bowler wiring inward wisdom preview
3 Hardware Workable Weakness Endowment Two Window

Key lines 4–6 twice: first for speed, then for control. Follow the same procedures as lines 4–6 in the B drill above.

4 Wear a warm gown if it snows; the weather is raw.
5 The new lawn will grow when watered well at dawn.
6 It is wise to wire the news to the waiting woman.

Additional Drill

Key the following drill. Press ***Enter*** after each line.

1 He is not an honest senator; he does not fool me.
2 At the rodeo, Jo dropped the looped rope and lost.
3 In the gloom, the senior pilot spotted an airport.

Think control as you key each line. If you make more than two errors on a line, repeat it. Keep your eyes on the copy in the text as you key.

3 Jerome's cat ran to Mary's house and said meow!!
4 "Hello," said Jim. "How are you this fine day?"
5 "Help!" yells the old man as the bees followed.

6 If the dress is $35.95, why is the coat $125.75?
7 Take #33 and move it to #66. Move #66 to #1234.
8 Farber & Daughters is the name of my law firm.
9 The check was made out for at least $*******.99.
10 You scored 89% on the exam and 78% on the drill.

11 Now is the time (11:45) for you (Ginny) to move.
12 I make $6 per hour, but I would like to make $9.
13 Sixteen @ $1.23 and 57 @ $23.45 is far too much.
14 If hours = 40 and rate = $5.00 then gross = $200.
15 The equation was A = B + C + F + D + G + H + I + J.

16 Jerry thought that A < B and F < G and JK < JKL.
17 However, Tom knew that A > B and F > G and I > IK.
18 If you raise 2^2 the answer will be squared now.
19 Enter your last name on the line that follows: ______________________.
20 LET B = A + B + C / D * H * (HH - K) + (HH + JJ).

21 Go to http://www.uwec.edu for information on course availability.
22 IF GH < AN AND TH > HJ OR TY < TU MOVE TRY TO A.
23 There will be a reaction—perhaps not good—if you do that.
24 PRINT TAB[17] "PLAYER" TAB[34] "FG PERCENT"; FG
25 The #12 category weights 18#; the #7 category weighs 6#.

23.9 ONE-MINUTE TIMINGS

Goal: 30 WAM/2 errors

Take a 1-minute timing on each paragraph.

1 Barlow, a shrewd fellow, winked as he waited in the shadows. A whistle warned him of the slow walk of his fellow worker. As he wallowed in the warmth of that workshop, Will worked in the wild, blowing wind. Barlow was worthless.

4 Beneath the bridge in the brook, the bears bathed.
5 He is bitter and bleak; the dark banjo is broken.
6 A nimble rabbit blinks and nibbles bean blossoms.

7 Will Marlow wash in warm water that wool sweater?
8 With a white towel, Warren wiped the jeweled bowl.
9 If Win washes the new window, is he wasting water?

THINKING DRILL

Using the list below, key as many words as you can think of that begin with the letters given.

bo	wo
bi	wh

Key the words in a list. Key all the "bo" words first. Then go to the next set of letters. Try to think of at least 10. If you can think of 20 to 30 words, that's great.

9.12 ONE-MINUTE TIMINGS

Goal: 25 WAM with no more than 2 errors

- Take a 1-minute timing on each paragraph.
- If you finish a paragraph before time is up, start over.

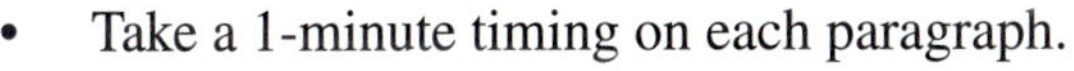

1 It is good to have honest goals. Nothing is gained if one goes forth in pointless roaming. A major effort is needed to prosper. Isolate those foolish errors and avoid them. Hold to a strong, firm hope and move along.

2 Floss shook in terror as the tornado stormed along the shore. The radio droned on foretelling doom and gloom. The phone popped in her ear as a torrent of rain fell. Alone in the old mansion, her fear overtook her for a moment.

3 Bif booked a berth on the battered boat. As he bragged to his somber brother, the boom of the harbor bells vibrated. Beneath the boasting, Bif began to babble. A belated bolt of disbelief and brooding stabbed at him.

4 Labor to do a noble job. Bosses like brains and ambition. A blend of both brings a desirable habit that boosts a beginner. A babbling boaster absorbs a bore. The absent laborer blemishes his possible bankroll boost.

5 We will await the word of warning in the new tower. The wise, stalwart leader wants to preview the writings of men of worth. He frowns on wrong narrow views. We will follow wise wishes and win a wearisome war and bestow a renewed foothold.

Less Than Sign Drill

The < symbol can be keyed with a space before and after it or with no space. Whichever you select, be consistent. Remember to use the left shift key, and anchor the "J" or the ";" finger for this reach. Key lines 1–3 twice for control.

1 2<7 3<8 4<9 5<6 8<9 1<2 5<7 6<8 k<l k<l 5<6 1<8<9
2 12 < 43 16 < 58 17 < 89 15 < 28 123 < 456 17 < 77
3 2 < 4, j < k, 1 < m, K < L; S < Z; K < L; JK < LM

Greater Than and Less Than Signs Drill

Follow the same spacing guideline as with the ***less than*** symbol. Key lines 1–3 twice for control. Anchor the "J" finger for this reach, and use the left shift key.

1 l<l l<l ;<; ;<; 6>4 6>2 5>1 9>7 l>l ;>>;;
2 L>M L>R ;>; 56 > 43 126 > 78 198 > 48 66 > 55 6>>
3 6 > 2 < 6; 6 > 1.2; 78 > 8; 1234 > 678; 56 < 234;

Forward Slash (Diagonal) Drill

The slash is used as a division sign in computer programming languages and in Web addresses such as http://www.emcp.com. It is also used to divide characters such as month, day, and year in the date (for example, 04/14/97).

Key lines 1–3 twice for control. Anchor the "J" finger when making this reach.

1 ;/; ;/; ;/; /;/ ;/; ;/; /;/ ;/; /;/ ;/ ;/ ;/;/ ;/
2 a = b/c d = f/g h=j/l t=k/j r = j / k fgh = rty/j
3 The equation: miles/hours will equal speed rate.

Backslash Key Drill

Key lines 1–3 twice for control. Anchor the "J" finger when making this reach.

1 The \ sign is used to designate a given file path.
2 For example, CD\ will return to the root directory.
3 The command, MKDIR\TGRADES, makes a DOS directory.

Specialized Punctuation Mark and Symbol Keys

All specialized symbols and punctuation keys presented in this unit are included in the 25 lines that follow. If you hesitate or are unsure of reaches on any of the drill lines, repeat the line.

Key each group of five lines once. If you need more practice, choose one or two groups to key again.

1 Two-thirds of the three-fourths are very gifted.
2 John said: Data Structures is a great textbook.

6 Will reviewed the written words. He did not wish to show that witless newsman how shallow his words were. However, he wanted to warn the world of the wasted wealth in the wages of the man. He showed the network the handwriting on the wall.

Ending the Session

Now you may print this session's files, continue to the next session, or exit the program. See page 24 of Session 6 if you need to review procedures.

Ergonomic Tip

Experiment with your foreground and background screen colors to find the combination that is most comfortable for you. Avoid using light-colored characters on the screen. Use dark characters on a light-colored background.

Session 23 EXPONENT, LESS THAN, GREATER THAN, DIAGONAL, BACKSLASH

Session Goals

^, <, >, /, \

Symbols

1-Minute: 30 WAM/2 errors
3-Minute: 25 WAM/2 errors

23.1-23.7 On-Screen Exercises: Getting Started

If you exited the program at the end of the previous session, refer to page 71 of Session 18 to review how to open the next session or to continue from where you left off.

23.8 Textbook Exercises: Reinforcement

This section provides a review of the proper reaches to the exponent sign, less than sign, greater than sign, slash/diagonal, and the backslash keys. When you have finished the drills, click Print (if desired), then Next Exercise.

Reviewing the Exponent Sign, Less Than, Greater Than, Diagonal, and Backslash

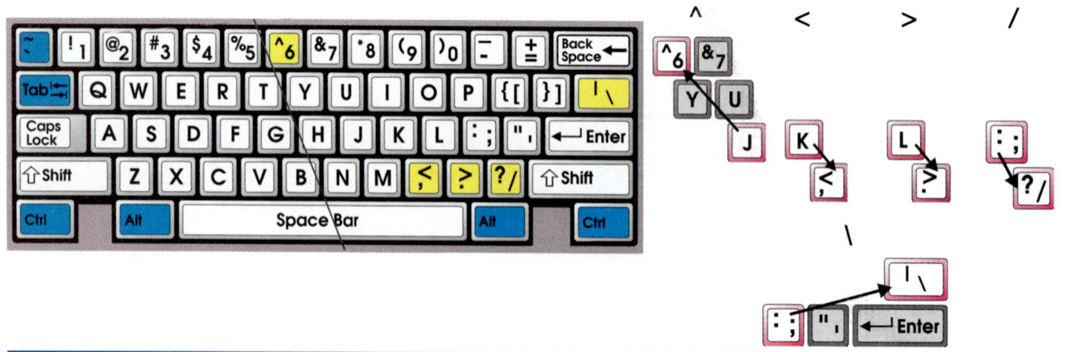

Exponent Sign Drill

Key lines 1–3 twice for control. Anchor the ";" finger when making this reach.

1 j6j j6j j6j j^j j^j j^j j^j J^J J^J J^J J^J J^J J^

2 The ^ sign is used to raise an integer to a power.

3 For example, 2^2 is the square of the numeral two.

Session 10

REINFORCEMENT: SESSIONS 1–9

Session Goals

Review keys from Sessions 1–9

25 WAM/2 errors

10.1 On-Screen Exercises: Getting Started

If you are continuing immediately from Session 9, you are already warmed up and are looking at Exercise 10.2. Click the Next Exercise or Previous Exercise button if you are not at the correct exercise. The copy for Exercises 10.2 – 10.4 is in your text. Exercise 10.2 consists of two 1-minute timings. Instructions to complete the timings and page number are shown on your screen.

If you exited the program at the end of the previous session, refer to page 11, Session 3 for instructions on entering the program.

10.2 CHECKING YOUR SKILL: ONE-MINUTE TIMING

In Sessions 7–9 you completed a series of 1-minute timings. Before you take the 1-minute timing that follows, check your scores on the Student Report. See page 27, Session 7 to review the instructions for viewing your report.

Goal: 25 WAM with 2 or fewer errors

1 When the winter snow thaws, warm rain washes the world. Wild flowers begin to weave in a slow swing with the wind. Whiffs of a meadow awakened swirl down at the dawn. The dew is a rainbow and twinkles as a jewel. Winter has blown onward.

10.3 Textbook Exercises: Reinforcement

The Special Drills that follow provide additional practice on the keys that you have learned in Sessions 1–9. However, if you are already keying over 25 WAM with no more than 2 errors and do not hesitate when keying, click the Next Exercise button three times. This will take you to Session 11, Exercise 2. If you are not at the 25 WAM with 2 or fewer errors level, proceed with the Special Drills to build speed and/or accuracy. When you have finished the drills, click Print (if desired), then click Next Exercise.

Here are guidelines for choosing drills:

1. If you have not mastered a key reach (you hesitate before striking the key), key the speed-building lines.
2. If you are not keying at least 25 WAM, key the speed-building lines.
3. If you are making more than 2 errors per minute, key the accuracy-building lines. If you make more than two errors on a line, key it again.

1 Symbols are used frequently in computer programming languages. Of course, the plus (+), minus (-), and equals (=) keys are used. The asterisk (*) is used as a multiplication sign, and the diagonal (introduced in the next session) is used for division. It is important that we key symbols just as quickly as we key numbers and letters.

2 Global area networks (GANs) are critical in today's business world. Many U.S. companies are selling their products in overseas markets. It is imperative that communication channels are established with branches, suppliers, and customers wherever they may be. Communication must be instant if a company is to remain competitive.

22.9 THREE-MINUTE TIMINGS

Goal: 25 WAM/2 errors

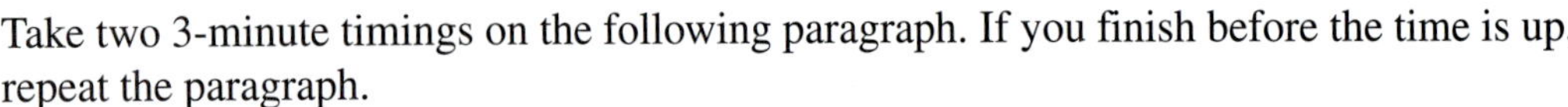

Take two 3-minute timings on the following paragraph. If you finish before the time is up, repeat the paragraph.

1 There is a new way to lay out a great garden that uses grids of neat 1-foot by 1-foot squares. Then, you plant the seeds and plants with certain spacings. The system is a simple one that allows persons to make the most of a garden space and at the same time conserve water and labor. Talented experts feel that 1-foot by 1-foot garden schemes let you grow the same amount of food as a regular garden does in less than one-fifth of the space.

Ending the Session

Now you may print this session's files, continue to the next session, or exit the program. See page 75 of Session 18 if you need to review procedures.

Ergonomic Tip

Use a desk lamp (task lighting) instead of overhead lights to eliminate screen glare.

Special Drills

- Key each line once.
- If you need more work on speed or accuracy, key the appropriate group of lines again.

Keys Review (Speed)

1 asdf jkl; ;p; frf jmj fvf lol fbf sws pr mv db wm
2 p pad pan peg pen pin pit pie plan phase pledge plane
3 r rap ran red rip rent rests real repels refers roam rope

4 m ham hem men him mate mind mesh manage mandate
5 v vat vim vet vise vent vane vigil valid veneer voter rigor
6 o oh or odd old one oaf opens omit ogle oval of oblong

7 b bad beg bid bop brag blend board brake better bowl
8 w was wed who win woe were when went where with
9 Shanon Olan Bronson George Janet Kent Martin John

Balanced-Hand Words (Speed)

1 lamb blend bland blame amble emblem problem bible
2 lap nap pen paid pane flap span pale spent dispel
3 air pan sir risks lair heir pair hair flair widow

4 map maid mane melt sham lame mend firm make flame
5 vie via pair vivid pelvis disown pens laps disown visit
6 fog sod oak rod foam fork form foam odor soak rod

7 bow wig wow vow down gown wisp with wish when wit
8 Did the lame lamb amble down to the big pale oak?
9 The pale widow paid for the vivid gown and a wig.
10 When did Vivian mend the pair of problem emblems?

Two-Letter Combinations (Speed)

1 pe peg pen pest pets pert peso petite petition
2 pi pin pie piles pipes pink pine pig piston pivot
3 That petite person with pets had piles of pinkish pills.

Equals Sign Drill

Key lines 1–4 twice for control. Anchor the "J" finger when keying the equals sign.

1 .;=; ;=; ;=; ;=; ;=; ;=; ;=; ;=; =;= =;= =;= =;= ;=
2 a = b c = d e = f g = g j = j k = k l = l ;=; ;=;;
3 A = D C = D J = J K = K L = L A = B C = D E = R =;
4 The = sign is generally used in math problems now.

Plus Sign Drill

Key lines 1–4 twice for control. Remember to press the ***left Shift*** key for the plus sign. Again, anchor the "J" finger when making this reach.

1 ;=; ;+; ;+; ;=+; ;+:+:+=; ;=; ;+; ;=; ;+; ;=; :+;
2 The equations were: A = D + F + G and E = E + RT.
3 The equations were: A = B + C + E and A = A + BC.
4 The computer program stated A = (B + C + C) * AD.

Additional Drill

Key lines 1–9 once for control. Press ***Enter*** after each line.

1 s2@s s@2s s2s s@s S@S S@S S@S s@s s@s s2s s@s
2 23 @ $2.31, 172 @ $8.91; 17 @ 57, 98 @ 34, 8,934 @ 90, 2 @ 4
3 dsmith@emcp.net; phantom@emcp.net; tmodl@emcp.net

4 =; =;= =;= =;= ;=; ;=; =;= =;= ;=; ;=; = =
5 a=b c=d e=f G=J H=I K=L m=n o=p q=r
6 The = sign is used in formulas when working in spreadsheets.

7 ;+; ;=; ;+; ;=; ;+; ;=; ;+:+:=; ;=+; :=+: :+=:
8 The formula A = C + BA is the same as A = (C+BA).
9 The spreadsheet formula stated D1 = (B2 + C3 + A1) * F4.

22.8 ONE-MINUTE TIMINGS

Goal: 30 WAM/2 errors

Take a 1-minute timing on each paragraph.

4 ra ran rap ranks rake rates raised range rapid random
5 ri rid rip rises ripe right ridges rigid rinse rigs rim
6 Rapid Red ran to the raised ridges on that range.

7 ma man mat math make mail marsh manager margin
8 mi mid mild mind mint midst might misting mire mite
9 The manager might mail the mild mints to the man.

10 va van vat vane vases vast valid varied vanish valve
11 vi vie vim vise vile vine visits vital vintage vision
12 The vital vintage vases vanished from a vast van.

13 oa oak oats oath oatmeal load toad roast float oasis
14 The oath at the oak tree oasis was about oats.
15 ba bad bag bail balk bath badge barks bandages bald

16 bl blade bleak blast blank blight blind blinks blow
17 The bat blinked at a baboon blinded in bandages.
18 wa was war wag wade wait wane wash waste waves wave

19 wi win wit wig wide wipe will wise wield wiper window
20 Winna washed and wiped her window; she wasted water.

Double-Letter Words (Accuracy)

1 slipping sipping happen flipping appease shipping
2 terriers irritates terrains follow all narratives
3 dimmer dinners hammering manners immense immerges

4 moon roof pool hood hook loot took mood root door
5 gobble rabble hobble babble pebble nibbles rabbit
6 of off offers offends offset offense offensive offering off shore

7 Janell slipped the irritated terrier in the door.
8 That immense rabbit followed and nibbled a bottle.
9 She will be shipping the poor winter winner soon.

Session 22

AT, EQUALS, AND PLUS SIGNS

Session Goals

@, =, +

Symbols

1-Minute: 30 WAM/2 errors
3-Minute: 25 WAM/2 errors

22.1-22.6 On-Screen Exercises: Getting Started

If you exited the program at the end of the previous session, refer to page 71 of Session 18 to review how to open next session or to continue from where you left off.

22.7 Textbook Exercises: Reinforcement

This section offers a brief review of the proper reaches to the "at" sign, equals sign, and plus sign keys. When you have finished the drills, click Print (if desired), then Next Exercise.

Reviewing the At Sign, Equals Sign, and Plus Sign Keys

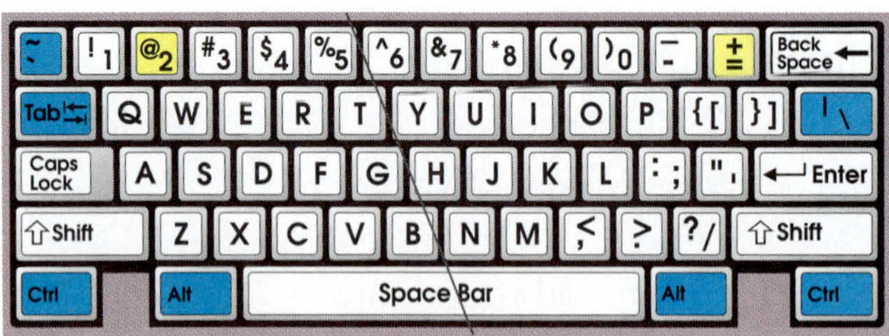

@

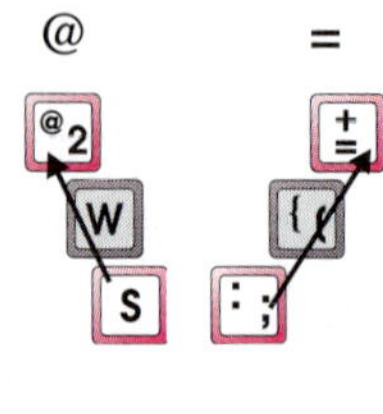

=

+

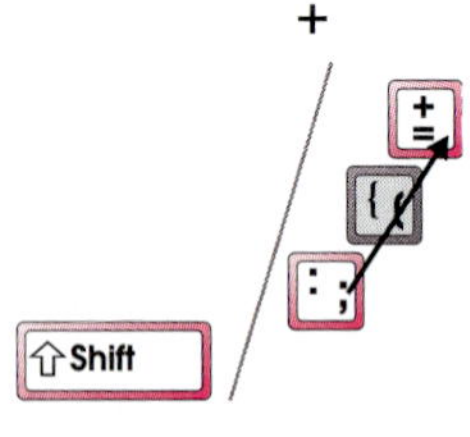

At Sign Drill

Key lines 1–4 twice for control. Be sure to press the ***right Shift*** key. Anchor the "f" finger when keying the "at" sign.

1 .s2s s2s s2s s2s s2s s2s s2s s@s s@s s2@s s2@s
2 14 @ $2.50, 16 @ $55.80, 1 @ $17.59, 13 @ $124.66
3 It is better to buy 99 @ 18 rather than 180 @ 10.
4 jjones@emcp.net; Xavier@emcp.net; vang@emcp.net

In the next three sets of drills, watch your finger make the reach from the home row to the sumbol key the first three times it is struck. Then concentrate on keeping your eyes on the copy to gain speed.

Longer Words (Accuracy)

1 elephant dependent safekeeping plaintiff pipeline
2 standard registrar parenthesis telegrams resident
3 That resident registrar sends standard telegrams.

4 familiar eliminate sentimental dependent estimate
5 retrieve primitive advertising privilege negative
6 Eliminate that sentimental, familiar advertising.

7 rational tradition imagination negotiate renovate
8 ambition elaborate observation establish possible
9 stalwart knowledge handwriting wholesale whenever
10 Establish rational imagination whenever possible.

10.4 ONE-MINUTE TIMINGS

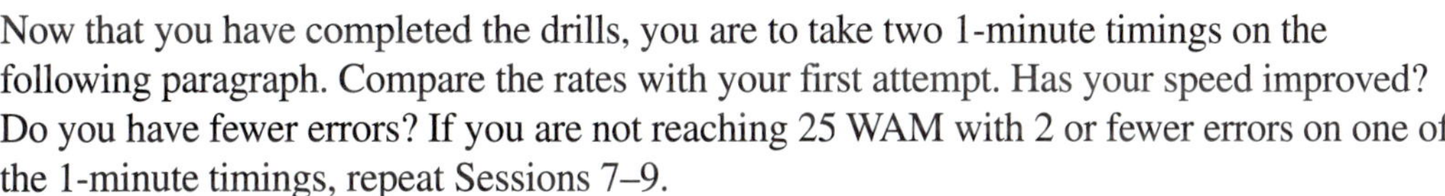

Now that you have completed the drills, you are to take two 1-minute timings on the following paragraph. Compare the rates with your first attempt. Has your speed improved? Do you have fewer errors? If you are not reaching 25 WAM with 2 or fewer errors on one of the 1-minute timings, repeat Sessions 7–9.

1 When the winter snow thaws, warm rain washes the world. Wild flowers begin to weave in a slow swing with the wind. Whiffs of a meadow awakened swirl down at the dawn. The dew is a rainbow and twinkles as a jewel. Winter has blown onward.

Ending the Session

Now you may print this session's files, continue to the next session, or exit the program. See page 24 of Session 6 if you need to review procedures.

As noted, repeat Session 7–9 if you didn't reach 25 wam with 2 or fewer errors. Without these skills, it will take you longer to master keyboarding.

Ergonomic Tip

Place paper copy on a copyholder rather than flat on the work surface so you are focusing directly on the copy.

1 Firms from which persons order items have to charge an amount for shipping and handling. Many firms do pay for the shipping amount if the items you ordered weigh less than a certain amount. If you have to pay the charges, you may wish to have that order sent by UPS. UPS uses varying charges according to the zone in which you live. UPS now has 8 mailing zones. Zone 1 is on the West Coast and Zone 8 is on the East Coast with all the rest of the zones located between these two points.

Ending the Session

Now you may print this session's files, continue to the next session, or exit the program. See page 75 of Session 18 if you need to review procedures.

Ergonomic Tip

Rest your forearms on the edge of a table. Grasp fingers of one hand and gently bend back wrist for five seconds to relax your hand and fingers.

Session Goals

U, Z, C

1-Minute: 25 WAM/2 errors

-ed and -ing word endings

11.1-11.10 **On-Screen Exercises: Getting Started**

If you exited the program at the end of the previous session, refer to page 11 of Session 3 to review how to open the next session or to continue from where you left off.

11.11 **Textbook Exercises: Reinforcement**

Some of the drills presented earlier on the computer screen are repeated here to reinforce your keyboarding skills, along with some new drills. When you have finished keying them, click Print (if desired), then Next Exercise.

Reviewing the U, Z, and C Keys

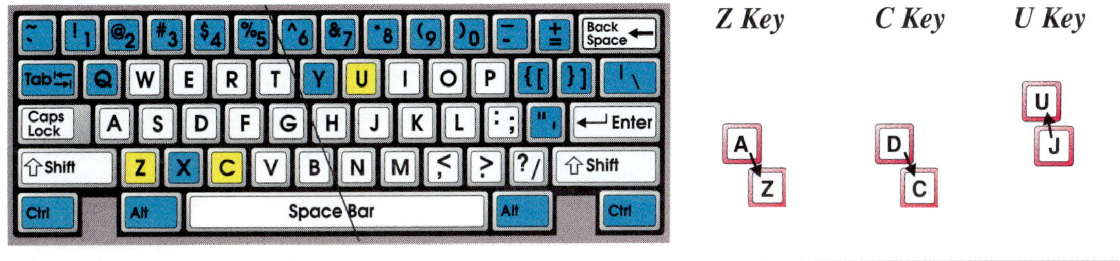

U Drill

Key lines 1–3 once, pushing for speed.

1 ju put put sun sun fun sun mud mud gum gum sum sum
2 vault audit rumor truth about nurse sprung refund blunt
3 Fusion Lawful Nature Urgent Plural Module Suppose

Key lines 4–6 twice: first for speed, then for accuracy.

4 Just be sure to return that blouse to the bureau.
5 That auto bumper is a hunk of junk; it is ruined.
6 A stout runner shouted and slumped to the ground.

Additional Drill

Key the following drill. Press ***Enter*** after each line.

1 k* K*K k*k k8*k k8k*k k*k*k k8*k k8*k k*k K*K k*k
2 The * symbol is used in formulas: A1*B2-C2*49.
3 f%f f5%f f%f f5%5 f5%f f5%f f5%f f%5f 5%5 5%5 555

4 Did you know that 5% of 5,000 equals 250% of 100?
5 ;[;[; ;[;[; ;[;[;[;[;[;[; ;[; ;[; ;[; ;[;; ;[; ;[;
6 ;];]; ;]; ;]; ;]; ;];]; ;];];];];]; ;]; ;]; ;]; ;]];

7 [;] [;] [;] [;] [;] [;] [;] [;] ;]; ;[; ;]; ;[; ;[;]
8 ;[; ;]; ;]; ;[; ;[; ;]; ;]; ;[; ;]; ;[; ;[; ;]; ;[; ;];
9 19 1(1 19L1 19(1 1(1 19(1 19(1 191 191 1(1 1(1

10 ;); ;0); ;0); ;0); ;); ;0); ;); ;); ;); ;); ;);(0)
11 The amount ($6.96) was more ($2 more) than I paid.
12 Most of the table (see Table 3.2) was accurate.

21.9 ONE-MINUTE TIMINGS

Goal: 30 WAM/2 errors

Take a 1-minute timing on each paragraph.

1 The stock market gets a lot of people's attention. When Standard & Poor's index increases, many people will hold on to their stocks in anticipation of further gains. A 4% drop in durable goods orders would most likely increase short-term interest rates; this has an impact on the Federal Reserve Board's next move.

2 The Radio Corporation of America (RCA) demonstrated the all-electronic 120-scan line television in the 1930s. In the same decade, Germany began regular TV broadcasting service. In the 1940s, coaxial (copper) cable was introduced as a more efficient method for telephone and television transmission. The progress in TV technology has been dynamic!

21.10 THREE-MINUTE TIMINGS

Goal: 25 WAM/2 errors

- Take two 3-minute timings on the following paragraph.
- Start the paragraph again if you finish before time is up.

Z Drill

Key lines 1–3 once, pushing for speed. Don't stop to correct errors unless directed by your instructor.

1 az maze maze doze doze raze raze zip zebra zest
2 seize breeze amaze razor hazel zombies wizard zing zane
3 Trapeze Zealous Pretzel Horizon Zealous Zenith

Key lines 4–6 twice: first for speed, then for control.

4 Liz seized that sizzling pizza and ate with zeal.
5 Minimize the hazard and stabilize that bulldozer.
6 Zeb baked a dozen pretzels in the sizzling blaze.

C Drill

Key lines 1–3 once, pushing for speed.

1 ca calk cane case calf camp carp cave cede cad came
2 camera notice impact circle decide zinc clock corner
3 Compare Produce Consult Service Council Enclosure Carl

Key lines 4–6 twice: first for speed, then for control.

4 Carlton, the cat, curled in comfort in the chair.
5 Chris decided to purchase a record and a picture.
6 Cecelia consumed a rich chocolate ice cream cone.

Additional Drill

Key the following drill. Press ***Enter*** after each line.

1 On the shrub in the puddle, Buff found a huge bug.
2 Sue slurps the sour soup as she slumps and sulks.
3 During the stunt, the group hummed a rousing tune.

4 Hazel won the prize as Buzz gazed with amazement.
5 The freezing drizzle glazed the bronze zinnias.
6 Hal has been penalized after embezzling a zillion.

7 With tonic and citric acid, can Carrie cure colds?
8 Could the clever client conceal crucial evidence?
9 A crow circled the cottage as Carol watched with caution.

Key each line for control; if you make more than two errors, repeat the line. Be sure to keep your eyes on the copy in the text as you key.

Asterisk Drill

In addition to signaling a footnote or indicating spacing, the asterisk serves as a multiplication sign in some programming languages. Anchor a finger on the "J" or ";" key to make the reach to the asterisk key.

Key lines 1–4 twice: first for speed, then for control. (Remember to press the ***left Shift*** key.)

1 k8k k8k k8k ki8k ki8k ki8*k k*k K*K k*k k*k *ki*k
2 8*8 8*8 8*8 k8*k ki8*k k*k 8*8*8 *** 8*8 ki8* k*k
3 The check was for $***4.65 and it should be $.46.
4 The * symbol is used in programming: A - B * 38.

Left Parenthesis Drill

Key lines 1 and 2 twice: first for speed, then for control. (Remember to press the left shift key.) Anchor your finger on the "J" key.

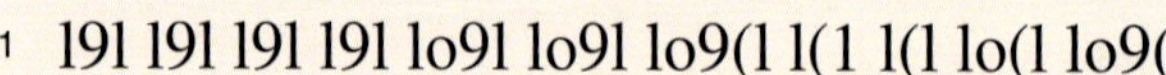
1 l9l l9l l9l l9l lo9l lo9l lo9(l l(l l(l lo(l lo9(

2 l(l l(l l9l l9l l9(l lo9(l lo(l lo9(l l9Ll l(l l9

Be sure to use the letter "l" and not the number "1" in this drill.

Right Parenthesis Drill

Key lines 1–4 twice: first for speed, then for control. (Remember to press the left shift key.) Anchor your finger on the "J" key.

1 ;0; ;0; ;0; ;0; ;p0; ;p0; ;p0; ;p0; ;p); ;p); ;0;
2 ;); ;); ;); ;); ;); ;0); ;); ;0); ;p0); ;p0); ;);
3 The price ($5.95) was more ($2 more) than I paid.
4 Most of the teams (at least 6) won all six games.

Students in Online Classes

Watch your little finger make the reach the first three times you key the bracket, then look at the text for the remainder of the drill.

Left Bracket Drill

Key lines 1 and 2 twice: first for speed, then for control. (Do not use the shift key.) Anchor your finger on the "J" key.

1 ;[; ;[; ;[; ;[; ;[; ;[; ;[;[;[;[;[; ;[;[; ;[;[;
2 ;[;[;[;[; ;[;[; ;[;[; ;[;[;[; ;[;[; ;[; ;[;[;

Left and Right Brackets Drill

Key lines 1 and 2 twice for control.

1 ;[; ;]; ;[; ;]; ;[; ;]; ;]; ;[; ;]; ;[; ;[; ;];];
2 ;[ ]; ;[; ;]; ;[; [;] [;] [;] [;] [;] [;] [;] [;]

11.12 ONE-MINUTE TIMINGS

Goal: 25 WAM with no more than 2 errors

Take a 1-minute timing on each paragraph.

1 The blunt auditor suggested to Duke that the business returns were a fraud. The usual routine of minimum turnovers of funds had been sound, but that fortune of thousands paid to a juror had not been inserted in the annual input. Duke presumed he was ruined and flushed with guilt.

2 Ruth sulked as her aunt poured a dose of the awful blue fluid. The sour stuff was supposed to be used for fatigue from the flu. She paused for a minute and gulped it down. Her aunt found four lumps of sugar for a bonus. Sullen disgust would turn into a laugh as a result.

3 Zeb zipped to that zoo with zest and nuzzled the zebras. He sneezed in the breeze and went to see the lizards. He wants to be a zoologist when he gets older. He knows a zillion things and his dazed and puzzled parents are amazed.

4 Zelda gazed in amazement as Zip, the wizard, seized a wand. It was ablaze with a maze of fire and lights. He did dozens of hazardous feats and puzzled all at the bazaar. He also was a trapeze whiz and dazzled folks.

5 A cookout on the beach could include cheese, carrots, meat sandwiches, and cold juice. If the chill of the ocean is too much, hot chocolate and hot coffee can chase the cold chills. The decent lunch and a chat with chums can enrich affection.

6 An office clerk who lacks basic ethics could become the subject of scorn. Those persisting in cruel and careless attacks on certain new workers can cause havoc. It is logical to follow strict, concise rules concerning office tact. Choose the right track and be sincere.

ENDING THE SESSION

Now you may print this session's files, continue to the next session, or exit the program. See page 24 of Session 6 if you need to review procedures.

Ergonomic Tip

Position your copyholder about the same distance from your eyes as the monitor so that your eyes don't have to refocus with different distances.

PERCENT SIGN, ASTERISK, PARENTHESES, BRACKETS

Session Goals

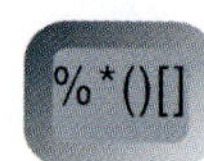

%, *, ( ), [ ]

Symbols

1-Minute: 30 WAM/2 errors
3-Minute: 25 WAM/2 errors

21.1–21.7 On-Screen Exercises: Getting Started

If you exited the program at the end of the previous session, refer to page 71 of Session 18 to review how to open the next session or to continue from where you left off.

21.8 Textbook Exercises: Reinforcement

This section offers a brief review of the proper reaches to the percent sign, asterisk, left and right parentheses, and left and right brackets keys. When you finish the drills, click Print (if desired), then Next Exercise.

Reviewing the Percent Sign, Asterisk, Brackets, and Parentheses Keys

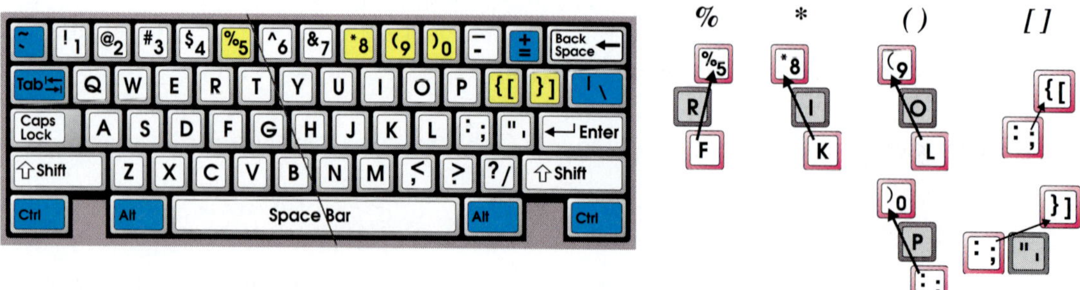

Percent Sign Drill

Be sure to press the ***right Shift*** key. Place both hands on the home row and practice the move from ***f*** to ***percent sign.*** Be sure to anchor your left little finger to the "A" key.

Key lines 1–4 twice: first for speed, then for control.

1 f5f f5f f5f f5f f5f f%f F%F f5f F%F5 f%f5 f%f f%f
2 55% 555% 5% 5%5% 555% 55% 5% 5% 55% 555% 5%, 555%
3 A 6% discount and a 10% reduction will equal 16%.
4 They made 55% of their shots and 8% of the fouls.

Session 12 Y, X, Q

Session Goals

Y, X, Q

1-Minute: 25 WAM/2 errors

Y and Q words

12.1-12.10 On-Screen Exercises: Getting Started

If you exited the program at the end of the previous session, refer to page 11 of Session 3 to review how to open the next session or to continue from where you left off.

12.11 Textbook Exercises: Reinforcement

Earlier in the session you completed new-key drills presented on the screen. Now you will repeat some of those drills, along with some new ones, to reinforce your keyboarding skills. When you have finished the drills, click Print (if desired), then Next Exercise.

Reviewing the Y, X, and Q Keys

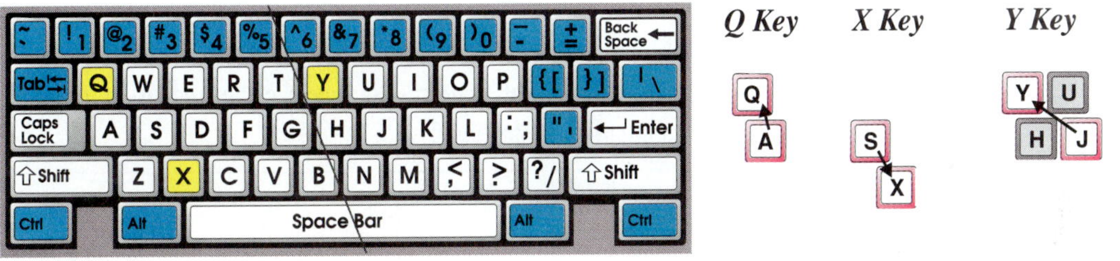

Y Drill

Key lines 1–3 once, pushing for speed.

1 jy yard play yowl very yolk away lazy sly yield yam
2 spray dairy entry handy lucky staying yonder young
3 Yearn Decay Empty Forty Hurry Lousy Playing Yale Taylor

Key lines 4–6 twice: first for speed, then for control.

4 The kitty and the puppy may not enjoy happy play.
5 It is only your duty to obey every law of safety.
6 Billy is ready to carry the heavy load Wednesday.

20.9 THREE-MINUTE TIMINGS

Goal: 25 WAM/2 errors

Take two 3-minute timings on the following paragraph.

1 Why should seat belts be fastened when a car is moving? Seat belts will reduce injuries and deaths. Many tests and studies have been done to prove this point. Half of all the traffic deaths happen within 25 miles from home. Traffic deaths can occur when an auto is moving just 40 miles an hour or less. If a car is moving at 30 miles per hour, the impact is like hitting the ground after hurtling from the top of a building that is three stories high.

Answers to Exclamation Point Drill B

Congratulations! You won the first prize.

Jan shouted, "What a mess!"

I emphatically restate my position: I will not resort to underhanded tactics!

Help! Help! I'm locked in.

Oh, how ridiculous! He's never even seen the inside of a bank.

Ending the Session

Now you may print this session's files, continue to the next session, or exit the program. See page 75 of Session 18 if you need to review procedures.

Ergonomic Tip

If you are experiencing eye pain, flashes of light, floaters, blind spots, or blurred vision, make an appointment immediately with a qualified professional.

X Drill

Key lines 1–3 once, pushing for speed.

1 sx axle next exam flex text hoax apex expedite fix fox
2 deluxe excise expand export prefix excite example
3 Explode Exhaust Examine Anxiety Exporting X ray Expert

Key lines 4–6 twice: first for speed, then for control.

4 Did excess oxygen explode during that experiment?
5 Explain the context and expedite that experiment.
6 Fix the exhaust and examine the axle of the taxi.

Q Drill

Key lines 1–3, pushing for speed.

1 aq quote quire squid quiet squaw query qualify quite
2 quench equate squeak equity squelching quit quartz
3 Squire Quarry Quaver Quorum Quartering Requesting

Key lines 4–6 twice: first for speed, then for control.

4 Do that quotient; it is a frequent quiz question.
5 Ducks squirmed and quacked in the squalid quarry.
6 Does the quitter frequently squabble and quibble?

Additional Drill

Key the following drill. Press ***Enter*** after each line.

1 In a sunny yard, the sassy gray puppy plays daily.
2 The friendly young boy, Gary, annoys Silly Sally.
3 A hungry baby in the subway was eyed by a sentry.

4 Examine her next; Maxine was exposed to smallpox.
5 The new relaxing exercise was explained in the textbook.
6 Is the lynx a vexing jinx or is it an exotic pet?

Think control as you key the sentence on each line. If you make more than two errors on a line, rekey the sentence. Remember to keep your eyes on the text as you key.

General Guidelines for the Exclamation Point

1 The exclamation point is used to express a high degree of emotion or strong feeling.
2 The exclamation point may be used in any of these situations:
   a *One word (space once after the exclamation point)*
      What! You mean the flight has been delayed for six hours?
   b *A phrase (space once after the exclamation point)*
      How frightening! The fire broke out only 10 minutes after we had left.
   c *A clause*
      The date of the meeting—mark it on your calendar!—is November 10.
   d *A sentence (space once after the exclamation point)*
      So there you are, you rascal!
   e *A quotation that is exclamatory*
      My brother yelled, "Run for your life!"
   f *A complete sentence that is exclamatory*
      I simply do not believe the fiscal report that states, "The absentee rate was increasing by 500 percent"!

Exclamation Point Drill B

Key each sentence, inserting appropriate punctuation. Answers are shown on page 86.

Congratulations You won the first prize
Jan shouted What a mess
I emphatically restate my position: I will not resort to underhanded tactics
Help Help I'm locked in
Oh, how ridiculous He's never even seen the inside of a bank

20.8 ONE-MINUTE TIMINGS

Goal: 30 WAM/2 errors

Take a 1-minute timing on each paragraph.

1 State, county, and regional fairs provide wholesome entertainment for more than 150 million Americans each year. The Texas State Fair has an annual $160-million-dollar impact on the Dallas-Fort Worth area with more than 3.1 million attendees. From animals to high-tech displays, there's something for everyone, and the price is right!

2 When ordering team jerseys, be sure to include #223-852 in the category box on the order form. JB & K provides an additional 5-percent discount for orders in excess of 15 jerseys. There is a significant savings on two-color jerseys compared to those with three or more colors. Prices are listed on the attached sheet.

7 The unique antique aquarium had a thick lacquer on it.
8 In the old square, the quake left queer quagmires.
9 The queasy squirrel was quarantined in the square box.

12.12 ONE-MINUTE TIMINGS

Goal: 25 WAM with no more than 2 errors

Take a 1-minute timing on each paragraph

1 Basically, employers like a loyal employee. Honesty and courtesy always pay off in any job or duty. Apathy and sloppy typing are always likely to be very costly to a company. Any employee who displays a steady style will be properly rewarded and enjoy a fairly large salary.

2 There is simply no key to easy money. A bad agency may say that you are lucky and a legacy of wealthy glory is yours. Yet, if you try fancy or phony schemes, you will be mighty sorry. Steady, weekly saving is the thrifty means to easy money. Lay a penny away a day and be happy.

3 An extra exercise to help your mind relax is inhaling and exhaling deeply. It extends all the oxygen capacity before it is expelled. Choose an exact time each day to expedite an extra relaxing exertion. Your anxieties and vexations disappear and you relax. Try this exciting experience.

4 Exercise an extreme caution before investing in an old duplex. Have an expert examine all the existing details and explain them to you. It may be easier to buy a luxurious and deluxe apartment house. An experienced land expert knows if it is an expensive venture.

5 The quick squad conquered the unique quintet without question. The quarterback squelched most questions about technique or quality of the team. If they qualify for the trophy, will they quietly squash the next team or will the coach require an extra practice session?

6 Angelique might request a price quotation on an exquisite antique quilt. She acquired it from a queen in a quaint town near the equator. Quiet inquiries have arisen from qualified buyers. The question is, should she keep the quality quilt or sell it quickly as requested?

Ending the Session

Now you may print this session's files, continue to the next session, or exit the program. See page 24 of Session 6 if you need to review procedures.

Ergonomic Tip

To sharpen the image, adjust the brightness/contrast controls on your computer screen.

Pound/Number Sign Drill

Key lines 1–3 once for control.

1 #33 33# 39 9# #168 168# #106 106# #3 3#3 21# #122
2 Items #10, #7, #3, #6, #4, #12, and #19 are mine.
3 Get #61 weighing 10# and #2299 weighing 189,756#.

Students in Online Classes

Note that the # sign has two meanings: pound and number. The # sign after a number represents pounds. The # sign before a number represents the word *number.*

Dollar Sign Drill

Key lines 1–3 once for control.

1 $1 $2 $3 $4 $5 $6 $7 $8 $9 $10 $11 $120 $16.00 f$
2 Add $1.16, $28.96, $17.44, $18.00, $21.13, $4.26.
3 The gifts cost $1.10, $6.90, $19.89, and $101.13.

Ampersand Drill

Key lines 1–3 once for control.

1 17 & 60 & 9 & 16 & 14 & 71 & 77 & 45 & 61 & 9891
2 Buy gifts from the J & K store and the R & Sons.
3 Contact Hart & Sons for the products you need.

Additional Drill

Key lines 1–12 for control. Press ***Enter*** after each line.

1 fff f4f ff ff f4f4 $$$ f$ f$ f4 f$ f$ f4 f4
2 $40.00 4$ $4.00 $$44 $4.00 $$44 44 $4 $4 f$f$ 444
3 $143,789.00 $1,640.68 $689.33 $17.31 $26.80 $1.44

4 d#d d3d# d#d# d#d# d3d3 ### d# d# d3 d# d# d3 d3
5 d#d d3#d #3 3# ##33 3# #3 ##33 33 #3 #3 3#3# 333
6 Buy 14#, 23#, 71#, 3#, 8#, 41#, 13#, 21#, and 6#.

7 j7j j7j& j&j& j&j& j7j7 &&& j& j& j7 j& j& j7j7
8 &j& j7j& j&j& && j7j& j7& &&77 77 &7 &7 7&7& 777
9 Patricia and Ron went to Samuelsons & Bigsby today.

10 a!a! a!a a!a a!a! a! a! a!a! a!a a!a a!a a! a! a!
11 What! How frightening! Mark your calendar!
12 My brother yelled, "Run for your life!" Wow!

While the instructions for the drills for the four symbol keys say to key each line once, repeat any line where you feel more practice is needed.

Session 13

REINFORCEMENT: SESSIONS 1–12

Session Goals

Review keys from Sessions 1–12

1-Minute: 25 WAM/2 errors

13.1 ON-SCREEN EXERCISES: GETTING STARTED

If you are continuing immediately from Session 12, you are already warmed up and are looking at Exercise 13.2. Click on the Next Exercise or Previous Exercise button if you are not at the correct exercise.

If you exited the program at the end of the previous session, refer to page 11, Session 3 for instructions on entering the program.

13.2 CHECKING YOUR SKILL: ONE-MINUTE TIMING

In Sessions 7–9 and 11–12 you completed a series of 1-minute timings. The speed and accuracy goals were presented at the beginning of each set of timings. Check your scores now by accessing your Timing Performance Report (See page 27 for instructions on viewing your report.)

Now take a 1-minute timing on the paragraph that follows, using your scores for the timings in Sessions 7–9 and 11–12 as benchmarks. If you didn't reach at least 25 WAM in those previous timings, push for speed. If you reached the 25 WAM goal but had more than 2 errors, work for accuracy. If you achieved both the speed and accuracy goals, push for even greater speed.

1 It is good to have honest goals. Nothing is gained if one goes forth in pointless roaming. A major effort is needed to prosper. Isolate those foolish errors and avoid them. Hold to a strong, firm hope and move along.

13.3 TEXTBOOK EXERCISES: REINFORCEMENT

The Special Drills that follow provide additional practice on the keys that you have learned in Sessions 1–12.

Reinforcing the Keying of Alphabetic Characters

At a clear screen, try these drills to improve your general keyboarding skills:

1. For locational security, key the entire alphabet, keying each letter twice (aa bb cc dd ee ff...). Repeat this process once or twice.
2. To develop your thinking-and-keying skills, key the alphabet backwards (z y x...).
3. Key the following sentence three times to practice all the letters of the alphabet:

Session 20 EXCLAMATION POINT, POUND SIGN, DOLLAR SIGN, AMPERSAND

Session Goals

!, #, $, &

Using exclamation points

1-Minute: 30 WAM/2 errors
3-Minute: 25 WAM/2 errors

20.1-20.6 On-Screen Exercises: Getting Started

If you exited the program at the end of the previous session, refer to page 71 of Session 18 to review how to open the next session or to continue from where you left off.

20.7 Textbook Exercises: Reinforcement

After reviewing the proper reaches to the symbol keys (exclamation point, pound sign, dollar sign, and ampersand), you will use these keys as you complete punctuation drills. Read the appropriate material in the text before you key each drill. When you are finished, click Print (if desired), then Next Exercise.

Reviewing the Symbol Keys

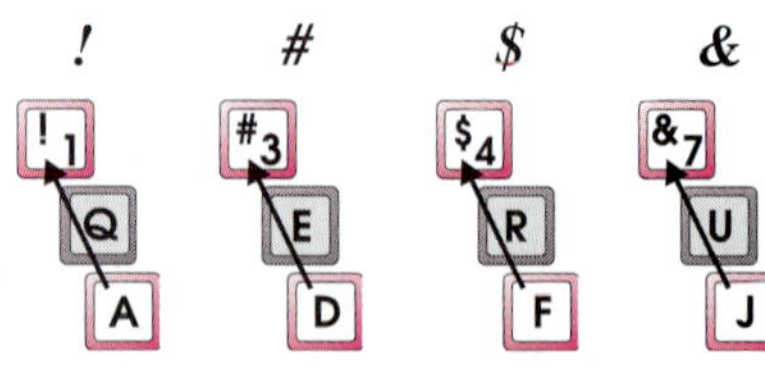

Symbols are located on the number keys. You have mastered the necessary reaches; now all you have to do is reinforce the location of each symbol. ***Remember:*** Be sure to press the ***Shift*** key.

Exclamation Point Drill A

Key lines 1–3 once. Space once after the exclamation point (except at the end of the line).

1 Help! Stop! No! Yes! Go! Wait! Begin! Halt! None!
2 Walter, stop right now! You had all better stop!
3 No, you cannot go right now! Listen to them now!

The quick brown fox jumped over the lazy dogs.

Repeat these drills whenever you can. They will help you master the alphabetic keys.

Assessing Your Skills

The drills that follow provide additional practice on the keys that you have learned. However, if you are keying over 25 WAM with no more than 2 errors and do not hesitate when keying, you may skip the drills and go to the next session by clicking the Next Exercise button three times. This will take you to Session 14, Exercise 2. If you have not achieved the 25 WAM or fewer than 2 errors level, proceed with the Special Drills to build speed and/or accuracy. When you have finished the drills, click Print (if desired), then Next Exercise.

Use the following guidelines to choose drills:

1. If you cannot key as rapidly as you would like (at least 25 WAM), key each line once of the Balanced-Hand Words drill.
2. If you have not mastered the reach to a key(s) (you hesitate before striking the key), key each line once of the Balanced-Hand Words, Letter Combinations, and Sentences with Letter Combination drills.
3. If you are making more than 2 errors per minute, key each line once of the Double-Letter Words and the Longer Words drills.

Balanced-Hand Words (Speed)

1 sign and the sigh ant sit ale elf hen end she and
2 then hang the and fig dig die tie did sit fit aid
3 fish sign than then lane lake lens hand than halt

4 lake idle half lens lane sign dish sign then disk
5 aisle island handle fight angle title shake snake
6 gland sleigh height fight slant digit angle eight

7 he and the elf and it if he an tight giant signal
8 amble bible problem blame bland blend lamb emblem
9 gown wig bow wow vow down wit when wish with wisp

10 flap pane paid pale spent dispel lap nap pen paid
11 foam fork form foal odor soak rod fog sod oak rod
12 heir lair risks sir pan air widow flair hair pair

13 pelvis disown pens laps vie via pair vivid flames
14 map mane maid melt sham lame mend firm make disks
15 The pale maid paid for the vivid title and a wig.

16 Did the pale lamb amble down to the big bland pen?
17 When did Bob sign the pair of problem emblems?

1 Fair time is near. Last year, our county had a great fair. Lots of people came to see the fine views and have a good time. Just imagine that 539,437 people attended, which was a record. We are hoping that by the next year we can have over 600,000 at the fair. The new rides were colorful and exciting. Both the young and old had a great time. We hope that the same old amusement company will come back and bring some of those new rides and fun shows that are bigger and better.

Answers to Quotation Mark Drills

"The computer is old," stated Mr. Barlow, "and must be replaced."

Why did the pilot say, "We'll be 30 minutes late"?

Catherine sleepily said, "Why don't you just be quiet?"

"We will be landing 30 minutes late," announced the pilot.

Deanna muttered, "I suppose that means we miss dinner."

The flight attendant smiled and said, "Perhaps we'll be on time after all."

The pilot announced, "Due to fog, we will be forced to land in Omaha instead of Minneapolis."

Deanna's fears were confirmed. "Omaha?" she blurted.

"Yes, it's a wonderful city. I vacation there often," replied the flight attendant.

The pilot was heard again, "We may not be able to leave Omaha for 36 hours. Be prepared to spend the night in the airport."

"An unexpected treat," said the smiling flight attendant.

The story was a real "corker."

The "gemot" was used largely in early English government.

With "friends" like you, who needs enemies?

A narrow path or ledge is sometimes called a "berm."

The poem entitled "Barney's Revenge" is not very long.

At midnight, Joan saw "The Light of Laughter" on television.

The author's last short story, "Bars on the Doors," was a mystery.

Her favorite song is "Thunder Serenade" by Mario Zahn.

Ending the Session

Now you may print this session's files, continue to the next session, or exit the program. See pages 75–76 of Session 18 if you need to review procedures.

Ergonomic Tip

Clean your monitor regularly with an anti-static screen cleaner recommended by the manufacturer.

Letter Combinations (Speed)

1 ta tall tan task taste tale take talk tag talent
2 th thesis thin theft this think than that then throw
3 te tenant tend tell tenth test tea tenor team

4 st stead steal steadiness stateside stag steam
5 sa sad saline Sal sang said sale sake safe sat sake
6 si since simple sinker sit single sift sip sin siphon

7 pe pets pest pen peg pea peat penguin pension
8 pi pine pink pipes piles pie pin pious pint
9 li like linkage linking link lien lied lie lid lime

10 le leaf least ledge lend lead left lest leap legacy
11 bl blade bleak blast blank blinds blind blight blow
12 ba bandages barks badge bath balk bail bag bad band

13 mi mire misting might midst mint mind milk mid
14 ma margin manager marsh mail make math mat man
15 oa float roast toad load oatmeal oath oats oak boat

16 ri rinse rigid ridges right ripe rises rip rid rice
17 ra rapid range raised rates rake ranks rap ran rayon
18 vi vintage vital visits vine vile vise vim vie viable

19 va vanish varied valid vast vases vane vat van varnish
20 wa waves waste wane wait wade wag war was wash wand
21 wi wiper wield wise will wipe wide wig wit win window

Sentences with Letter Combinations (Speed)

1 Janie washed and wiped her wig; she wasted water.
2 The boy blinked at a baby bound in bandages.
3 Those offensive oats floated off of that oatmeal.

4 The vital vintage vases vanished from a vast van.
5 The manager might mail the mild mints to the man.
6 Rapid Red ran to the raised ridges on that range.

Additional Drill

Key the following drill. Press ***Enter*** after each line.

1 ;';' ;';;';;';;';' ;' ;' ‘;';;';;';;' ;' ;'
2 can’t couldn’t John’s hat, people’s voice, anybody’s guess
3 Keat’s sonnets, girls’ clothes, 100’, 255’, they’re, it’s

4 ;”;” ; ” ;”;” ;”;;” ;” ;” ;”;;”;;”;;” ;” ;” ;'
5 “The weather is really nasty,” said Nancy.
6 When did you say, “I shall not return”?

7 She asked, “Do you know if the train is late?”
8 “The Midnight Ride of Paul Revere” is a good poem.
9 Marvin thought the concert was “far out” and enjoyable.

19.8 ONE-MINUTE TIMINGS

Goal: 30 WAM/2 errors

Take a 1-minute timing on each paragraph.

1 This new book on soccer has an excellent chapter on coaching soccer that offers 14 “awesome” tips to be used in working with young people new to the sport. There are some excellent suggestions on how to get positive support from the parents of the players. It’s a great resource for coaches and their assistants.

2 A personal computer’s components determine the limitations. For example, a computer without a video adapter and a video “codec” wouldn’t be able to store the filming done via a camcorder. What can be done with the right components in today’s microcomputers is amazing. It wouldn’t take long to think of 101 things that could be done on a computer with the “right” components.

19.9 THREE-MINUTE TIMINGS

Goal: 25 WAM/2 errors

- Take a 3-minute timing on the following paragraph.
- If you finish before time is up, start the paragraph again.
- Take a second 3-minute timing; try to increase your speed while maintaining your accuracy.

7 That person had piles of pipes for them.
8 Then that steady tenant, Ted, did a tenth strength test.
9 Steadfast Stacy talks a lot and stands as she talks.

10 Sad Sal sang a signal as she sighted a safe date.
11 At least lower the left lid and shorten the length.
12 That hanging kite tail brings the person around.

13 Gal, finish the gasket for the gas gadget game.
14 I dislike the heat dial that fits the dental fan.

Double-Letter Words (Accuracy)

1 seed teens needless feeling indeed needs glee see
2 tall stall knitting install little shall hall all
3 heel steed likeness dissent seeing sheet need fee

4 see feel teeth indeed gallant sledding sleet knee
5 hill still lifeless endless assist stiff kiss add
6 eggs stall eggshell falling haggle sniff sell egg

7 tell shell settling skilled allied skill fell add
8 deed sleek seedling fiddles needle sheen keen eel
9 rabble rabbit gobble nibbles pebble babble hobble

10 narratives all follow terrains irritates terriers
11 door root mood took loot hook hood pool roof moon
12 immerges immense manners hammering dinners dimmer

13 shipping appease flipping happen sipping slipping
14 of offensive offense offset offends offers off of
15 She will be stalling the nice contest winner now.

16 That immense rabbit emerged and nibbled a carrot.
17 Tu Wee slipped the irritated kitten into the house.

Longer Words (Accuracy)

1 negative retrieve primitive privilege advertising
2 estimate familiar eliminate dependent sentimental
3 Eliminate that sentimental, familiar advertising.

The pilot announced, Due to fog, we will be forced to land in Omaha instead of Minneapolis. Deanna's fears were confirmed. Omaha? she blurted. Yes, it's a wonderful city. I vacation there often, replied the flight attendant. The pilot was heard again, We may not be able to leave Omaha for 36 hours. Be prepared to spend the night in the airport. An unexpected treat, said the smiling flight attendant.

Using Quotation Marks in Titles and for Emphasis

1 Quotation marks are used to enclose titles of works such as poems; short stories; chapters, essays, or articles in magazines and other larger works; radio and television programs; and short musical works.

"The Midnight Ride of Paul Revere" is a good poem.
The last episode of "Star Trek" was really interesting.
The plot of "Last Rays of Daylight" was dull for a short story.
Did the band perform "Stardust" last evening?
I read the article "Thirty Ways to Avoid Work" in the magazine.

2 Quotation marks may be used within a sentence to give a word or words special emphasis, for example, a technical word used in a nontechnical sentence, slang expressions, humorous expressions, or defined words. (In typeset material, defined words are usually set in italics.) Be careful not to overuse the quotation mark in this manner.

The "Aglaonema" is commonly called the Chinese evergreen.
Marvin thought the concert was "far out" and enjoyable.
Their idea of "fast" service is serving one customer at a time.
According to Webster's dictionary, a wren is a "brown singing bird."

Quotation Mark Drill

Key each of the following sentences, inserting quotation marks to enclose titles or special words of emphasis. When finished, compare your results to those found on page 82.

The story was a real corker.
The gemot was used largely in early English government.
With friends like you, who needs enemies?
A narrow path or ledge is sometimes called a berm.

The poem entitled Barney's Revenge is not very long.
At midnight, Joan saw The Light of Laughter on television.
The author's last short story, Bars on the Doors, was a mystery.
Her favorite song is Thunder Serenade by Mario Zahn.

4 resident standard telegrams registrar parenthesis
5 pipeline elephant dependent plaintiff safekeeping
6 That resident registrar sends standard telegrams.

7 initiated hesitating alkaline likeness indefinite
8 delegates heightened lengthened stealing gaslight
9 The hesitating delegate is stealing the gaslight.

10 digital lenient distant inkling heading delighted
11 disliked endless athlete install flatten inflated
12 A lenient athlete has inflated the flattened keg.

13 whenever stalwart wholesale handwriting knowledge
14 renovate negotiate imagination tradition rational
15 possible establish observation elaborate ambition

16 Establish rational imagination whenever possible.
17 seashells tasteless steadfast thankless defendant
18 attendant delighted sightless lightness negligent

19 legislate essential stateside skinflint landslide
20 Seashells in the landslide delighted a skinflint.

13.4 REPEATING THE ONE-MINUTE TIMING

Now that you have finished the Reinforcement section, the next activity is to take two timings on the following paragraph. (Check your screen for specific information.)

1 It is good to have honest goals. Nothing is gained if one goes forth in pointless roaming. A major effort is needed to prosper. Isolate those foolish errors and avoid them. Hold to a strong, firm hope and move along.

Compare the results with your earlier attempt. Has your speed improved? Do you have fewer errors? If you are not reaching 25 WAM with 2 or fewer errors on the 1-minute timings, repeat Sessions 11–12.

Ending the Session

Now you may print this session's files, continue to the next session, or exit the program. See page 13 of Session 3 if you need to review procedures.

Ergonomic Tip

To minimize eye strain, align the computer monitor and keyboard directly in front of you.

19.7 TEXTBOOK EXERCISES: REINFORCEMENT—PART TWO

When you have finished the drills on quotation marks, along with the additional drills, click Print (if desired), then Next Activity.

General Guidelines for Quotation Marks

The three most common uses for quotation marks are to indicate conversations, to indicate emphasis, and to highlight titles in published material.

Using Quotation Marks in Written Conversation

1 Quotation marks are used to indicate spoken words in written materials. When each new speaker says something, the text begins on a new line and is indented. Study these examples:

  "The weather is really nasty," said Nancy.

  Relaxed, Jan yawned and said, "Oh, I really hadn't noticed."

  "That's because you have been sleeping all morning," murmured Nancy with a slight sneer in her voice.

2 The comma and period are placed inside the quotation marks. (See the previous examples.)

3 The question mark is placed either inside or outside the ending quotation mark, depending on the sentence logic.

  a Place outside if the entire sentence is a question.

    When did he say, "I shall not return"?

    Did he say, "I saw ten paintings at the exhibit"?

  b Place inside if the quotation **only** is a question.

    The owner shouted, "Why don't you just leave?"

    She asked, "Do you know if the train is late?"

4 The semicolon and colon **always** go outside the end quotation mark.

  Last week she announced, "Recreation time will be lengthened"; however, we have not experienced it yet.

Quotation Mark Drill

Now test your knowledge of quotation mark guidelines by keying the following sentences. (The correct answers are shown on pages 81–82.)

Key the three sentences, inserting quotation marks where appropriate.

The computer is old, stated Mr. Barlow, and must be replaced.
Why did the pilot say, We'll be 30 minutes late?
Catherine sleepily said, Why don't you just be quiet?

Key the following three sentences as conversation, adding quotation marks as appropriate.

We will be landing 30 minutes late, announced the pilot. Deanna muttered, I suppose that means we miss dinner. The flight attendant smiled and said, Perhaps we'll be on time after all.

Key the following as conversation, adding quotation marks as appropriate.

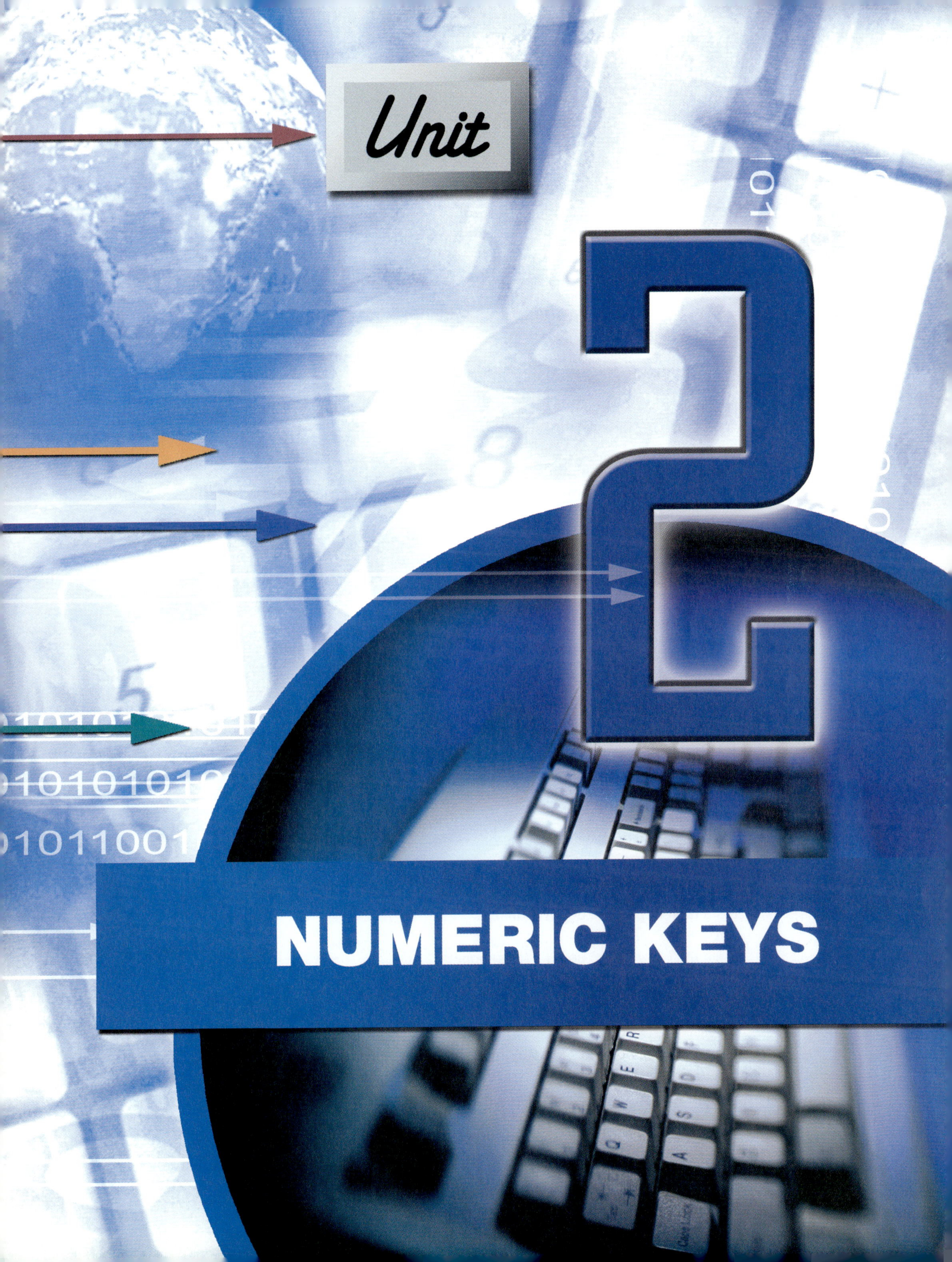
Unit
2
NUMERIC KEYS

Quotation Mark Drill

Key lines 1–3 twice: first for speed, then for control.

1 "hello" "Help" "gasp" "Fiddle" "Ha" "Hi" "splash"
2 "At last," said Sal, "is that lad's knee healed?"
3 "At least," said Al, "Jake ate the jelled salad."

19.6 On-Screen Activities: Thinking Drills

General Guidelines for the Apostrophe

1 An apostrophe is used in a contraction—a shortened spelling of a word, substituting an apostrophe for the missing letter.

cannot	can't
could not	couldn't

2 An apostrophe can be used to show possession by adding an 's.

a hat belonging to John	John's hat
the voices of the people	people's voices
the guess of anybody	anybody's guess

For plural nouns that end in s, add the apostrophe only.

the carts of the golfers	golfers' carts
the clothes of the girls	girls' clothes

3 An apostrophe can also be used as a symbol for feet.

100 feet	100'
255 feet	255'

Note: Some individuals have trouble determining if a word is a personal pronoun or a contraction.

Example: their they're its it's

Remember: The apostrophe indicates a missing letter. Therefore, *they're* indicates *they are,* and *it's* stands for *it is.*

Additional examples:

They're taking their own sleeping bags.
not
They're taking they're (they are) own sleeping bags.

It's a treat to give the dog its bone.
not
It's a treat to give the dog it's (it is) bone.

Thinking Drill

Now you have an opportunity to apply the apostrophe guidelines in a Thinking Drill. Follow the instructions on the screen. After you have completed the drill, return to the text and review the information that follows on using quotation marks correctly.

Session 14

1, 2, 3

Session Goals

1, 2, 3

1-Minute: 30 WAM/2 errors

Introduction

Session 14 is the first session on mastering the number row, located just above the alphabetic keys on your keyboard. Since numbers are used so frequently with the alphabetic keys and with many of the symbols (for example, the percent sign), developing equal skills with numbers, symbols, and letters is important.

14.1-14.5 On-Screen Exercises: Getting Started

If you are continuing immediately from Session 13, you are already warmed up so start with Exercise 14.2. Click on the Next Exercise or Previous Exercise button if you are not at the correct exercise.

If you exited the program at the end of the previous session, refer to page 11, Session 3 for instructions on entering the program.

14.6 Textbook Exercises: Reinforcement

Some of the drills presented earlier on the screen are repeated here to strengthen your keyboarding skills, along with some new drills. When you have finished the drills, click Print (if desired), then Next Exercise.

Keying Numbers

Whether you keyboard for personal or for business use, you will frequently key numbers. Some of the numbers that occur regularly in textual material include social security, telephone, address/ZIP Code/postal zone, age, weight, height, credit card, and driver's license numbers.

Reviewing the 1, 2, and 3 Keys

- Use the home-row method (anchor the left hand on asdf, the right hand on jkl;).
- Whenever possible, think of numbers in units of two and three digits (as you key 11, think eleven).
- When letters and numbers are combined, think of the letter(s) plus a two- or three-digit number (for a111, think ay/one-eleven).

Session 19 APOSTROPHE, QUOTATION MARK

Session Goals

Apostrophe, Quotation Mark

1-Minute: 30 WAM/2 errors

Using apostrophes
3-Minute: 25 WAM/2 errors

19.1-19.4 On-Screen Exercises: Getting Started

If you exited the program at the end of the previous session, refer to page 71 of Session 18 to review how to open the next session or to continue from where you left off.

19.5 Textbook Exercises: Reinforcement—Part One

After reviewing the proper reaches to the apostrophe and quotation mark keys, you will use these keys as you complete drills on keying word contractions, conversations, and titles of written works. Read the introductory material for each topic before you key the corresponding drill. When you have finished the drills, click Print (if desired), then Next Exercise.

Reviewing the Apostrophe and Quotation Mark Keys

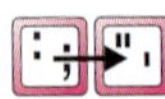

Apostrophe Drill

Key lines 1–3 twice: first for speed, then for control.

1 Al's Dad's Ted's Allen's Jane's Jan's Ken's Len's

2 Alfie's neat sedan hasn't had a dent; he's tense.

3 Dale's latest theft hadn't shaken Jeanne's faith.

Note that the apostrophe and the quotation marks are on the same key.

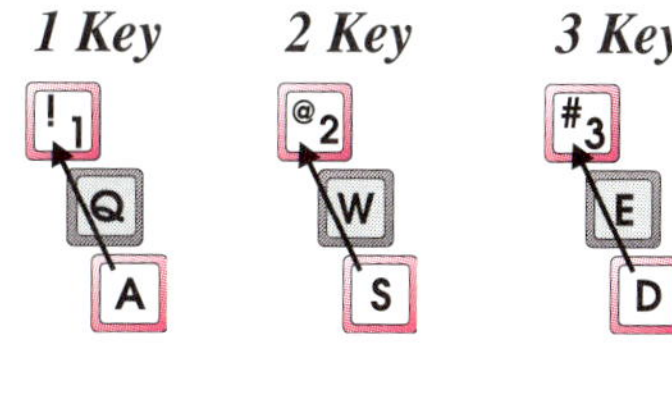

1 Key Drill

Key line 1 for control; key line 2 for speed. (Note that the lines contain the number 1, not the letter l.)

1 al lal alll al al all alll al llall al lal all al
2 all alll lla al lal all llla 111 lla 11 al lla la

2 Key Drill

Key line 1 twice for control; key line 2 twice for speed. Remember: when keying 21, think twenty-one, not two one.

1 1 2 1 21 221 122 121 221 2 1 212 112 1 12 21 21 2
2 al2 2al 112a 12al2 21al 122a all a2a 12a la2a 122

Note: Did you think of 221 as ***two-twenty-one***? Did you think of 112a as ***one-twelve/ay***?

Keying Numbers with Four Digits

When working with groups of numbers having four digits and no natural break, think of the numbers as two pairs.

Key lines 1 and 2; read the numbers in pairs to gain speed. As you key 1221 think twleve/twenty-one.

1 1221 1112 1221 1112 2112 2112 1122 1122 1221 2221
2 a1122 a1221 1112a 1212a a1112 a2112 a1212 a1221a2

Keying Numbers with Five or More Digits

When keying number groups that have more than four digits and no natural breaks such as spaces, commas, or decimals, use a 2-3-2 reading pattern. For the number 21221, think ***twenty-one/two twenty-one.*** For the number 2121221, think ***twenty-one/two-twelve/twenty-one.***

Key lines 1–5 once; mentally pronounce the number combinations as they are keyed.

1 21 221 21 221 21 221 a21 212a 12 11a 2121 a121 a2
2 21221 21121 21221 a21112 a12212 a12121 21212 a122
3 a2112121 22 1 21a 2122121 12221 a212a 1221a 12221

3. At the View Submissions Report Wizard, click Show session files to see the drill lines text (Exercises 18.1-18.8), or Show timings files to see the timings text (Exercises 18.9-18.10).
4. Click Show Report.
5. Click the name of the file you want to print.
6. At the Word Processor dialog box, click Launch.
7. Click File, and then click Print.
8. At the Print dialog box, click OK.
9. Click the Close button to close the Paradigm Word Processor.
10. Click Home on the Snap menu bar to return to the Welcome page.

Continue

To continue on the next session, click the Next Exercise button **twice**. This will take you to Exercise 19.2. (You will bypass Exercise 19.1 Warmup since you are already warmed up.)

Exit

To exit, do the following:

1. Click the Close button in the top right corner of the screen.
2. At your Paradigm Keyboarding with Snap Welcome page, click Logout.

Ergonomic Tip

Try using a document stand to hold your source materials—position it so that the distance from your eyes to the copy is the same distance as your eyes to the screen.

4 12 12 12 12 121 121 121 121 a2a a221 a221 2a211 1

5 212a1 121221a 12122a1 22221a 12212a 221221a 21a22

Remember: Keep your fingers on the home row and reach from that position to key a particular number or several numbers. Return your finger to the home-row position after striking a number.

3 Key Drill

Key lines 1–3. Repeat the lines, keeping your eyes on the copy while mentally reading the numbers as combinations.

1 332 32 213 231 12 1321 231 32 231 2312 232 1213 3

2 a33 a3 a32 a321 a233 a3232 a132 13232 3223212 a23

3 a323 a3212321 a13231a a1 231a a123 232 32 332 a13

Sentences

(Omit if Sessions 1–13 have not been completed.)

Key lines 1–3 once for speed.

1 Jean shall sell the 321 seashells and 212 stones.

2 Taste the lean tea; handle the kettle that leaks.

3 The 11 attendants halted a ring of thieves. They felt proud.

Key lines 4–6 once for control. Key lines 4–6 again. If you make a mistake on a line, start over until you can complete the line without error. Then go to the next line.

4 See, he is ill; his skin is flushed; he feels faint.

5 Enlist the 13 students to help with the many tasks.

6 She is a skilled athlete who strives for perfection.

Additional Drill

Key the following drill. Press ***Enter*** after each line. Remember to mentally read numbers with 2 or more digits in combinations.

Reading numbers in groups will help you gain speed and improve accuracy. This method is sometimes referred to as "syllabizing" numbers.

1 2 21 21 12 1 112 212 1 2 221 121 121 221 21 1 2 1

2 222 222 22 222 2 222 222 22 2 2 222 222 22 22 2 2

3 3 3 3 33 33 33 33 33 333 33 33 3 3 3 33 33 33 3 3 3

4 1231 3323 321 13 33212 323321 233 23 231 13 233 3

5 a22132213 a21321 2331 2a 22312a 231132a 323132112

6 3112 1232 3321 2311 3122 1312 3222 3221 1223 1233

7 23 3231 2231 123 121 233 32 12131 221312 31131 12

8 3123 123212 133132 123 321233 3112 32 132 1132 21

9 32 321 33312 12 3 23222123 1122331 12 1223 311132

18.10 ONE-MINUTE TIMINGS

Goal: 30 WAM, 2 errors

Take a 1-minute timing on each paragraph.

1 There has been a fantastic growth in the United States in the use of in-line roller skates, sometimes called Rollerblades, which is a trade name. People are using their in-line skates in conjunction with their employment. Couriers in New York City deliver their packages using their in-line skates to move quickly through the crowded streets. USA Hockey created an in-line hockey division in 1994.

2 Two-way radio systems are used by selected groups such as the police, ambulance services, and taxi cab companies. Users are limited to a single, manually selected channel. If the channel is in use, then the person must wait until it is free. There is no privacy for two-way radio systems; all others on your channel can listen to your conversation.

18.11 THREE-MINUTE TIMING

Goal: 25 WAM, 2 errors

So far all timings have been 1 minute long. Now you will take a 3-minute timing to help prepare you for keying longer documents such as reports. In most cases, speeds drop and errors increase when the length of the timing is extended. Your goal for this timed writing is to reach at least 25 WAM with no more than 2 errors per minute. Try to come within 5 WAM of your 1-minute rate while maintaining your accuracy at no more than 2 errors per minute. Remember to start over if you finish the paragraph before time is up.

1 Nails date back to 3000 B.C. They have been found in diggings and sunken ships that sailed in the years around 500 A.D. The Romans hand-forged nails and began the new trend toward complete use in building with wood. Most nails were first made in small shops; demand for nails grew so fast that the small, but well-made supply of handmade nails was not quite enough for the demand. Today, most companies that make nails can trace their own beginnings back to those early times.

ENDING THE SESSION

Now you may print this session's files, continue to the next session, or exit the program.

Print

To print Exercises 18.1 – 18.10 proceed as follows:

1 Click the Close ☒ button in the top right corner of the screen.
2 At your Paradigm Keyboarding with Snap Welcome page, point to Reports on the Snap menu bar, and click View Submissions Report.

14.7 ONE-MINUTE TIMINGS

Goal: 30 WAM with no more than 2 errors

Take a 1-minute timing on each paragraph.

1 When business is weak, there is not a lot of demand for money. So savings are invested in the stock market. The prices of stocks and bonds go up and interest rates go down. When business is strong, the demand for loans goes up to expand production, and consumers buy cars and homes. This pushes interest rates up.

3 The blunt auditor suggested to Duke that the business returns were a fraud. The usual routine of minimum turnovers of funds had been sound, but that fortune of thousands paid to the 12 jurors had not been inserted in the annual input. Duke presumed he was ruined and flushed with guilt.

Ending the Session

Now you may print this session's files, continue to the next session, or exit the program.

Print

To print Exercises 14.1 – 14.7 proceed as follows:

1. Click the Close button in the top right corner of the screen.
2. At your Paradigm Keyboarding with Snap Welcome page, point to Reports on the Snap menu bar, and click View Submissions Report.
3. At the View Submissions Report Wizard, click Show session files to see the drill lines text (Exercises 14.1-14.6), or Show timings files to see the timings text (Exercise 14.7).
4. Click Show Report.
5. Click the name of the file you want to print.
6. At the Word Processor dialog box, click Launch.
7. Click File, and then click Print.
8. At the Print dialog box, click OK.
9. Click the Close button to close the Paradigm Word Processor.
10. Click Home on the Snap menu bar to return to the Welcome page.

Continue

To continue on the next session, click the Next Exercise button **twice**. This will take you to Exercise 15.2. (You will bypass Exercise 15.1 Warmup since you are already warmed up.)

Exit

To exit, do the following:

1. Click the Close button in the top right corner of the screen.
2. At your Paradigm Keyboarding with Snap Welcome page, click Logout.

Ergonomic Tip

Sit in a slightly reclined position with thighs parallel to each other. In other words, do not cross your legs, as it cuts circulation.

18.9 Textbook Activities: Reinforcement

In the activities that follow, you will review the Underscore Key and do additional drills. When you are finished with the drills, click Print (if desired), then Next Exercise.

Reviewing the Underscore Key

Use the Underscore key on the keyboard when keying a blank line. Remember to hold down the ***Left Shift*** key.

Underscore Drill

To practice using the Underscore key, key lines 1–2 twice: first for control, then for speed.

1 The number of persons who will attend ____________________.
(Press underscore key 10 times—if you hold the underscore key down, you will get a continuous line until you release the shift key and the underscore key.)

2 Enter the street address here ________________. (Press underscore key 10 times.)

Additional Drill (hyphen, dash, underscore)

Key the following drill. Press ***Enter*** after each line.

1 ;-;- ;-; ;-; ;-; ;-;- ;- ;- -;-; ;-; ;-; ;- ;- ;-
2 ex-roommate, self-taught, vice-principal, one and one-third
3 sixty-six, a self-employed person, a last-minute effort
4 one hundred fifty-six, eight-cylinder engine, twenty-six

5 ;—; ;—; —;—; —;—; ;—; — — ;—; —;—; —
6 There is a flaw in the plan—a fatal one.
7 All books—fiction, poetry, and drama—are on sale.
8 I said once—and I will say it again—I disagree.

9 I cooked the meal—but they got the credit for it.
10 ;-;_ ;- _;_ _;_ — — ;__; ;-_ ; ;-_; ____ ;- ;_;_;_ ;-;_;
11 The book title is________________
12 Enter your name here_______________________

The dash can be presented two ways: two hyphens or space/hyphen/space. In this program, use two hyphens for a dash.

Session 15 — 4, 5, 6

Session Goals

4, 5, 6

Numbers (1-Minute): 25 WAM/2 errors
Letters (1-Minute): 30 WAM/2 errors

15.1-15.6 On-Screen Exercises: Getting Started

If you are continuing immediately from Session 14, you are already warmed up so start with Exercise 15.2. Click the Next Exercise or Previous Exercise button if you are not at the correct exercise.

If you exited the program at the end of the previous session, refer to page 11, Session 3 for instructions on entering the program.

15.7 Textbook Exercises: Reinforcement

Some of the Session 15 drills that were presented on-screen are repeated here, along with some new drills, to reinforce your sense of where keys are located. When you are finished with the drills, click Print (if desired), then Next Exercise.

Reviewing the 4, 5, and 6 Keys

4 Key

5 Key

6 Key

4 Key Drill

Key lines 1–3 twice: first key line 1 for speed, then key the same line for control. Do the same thing for lines 2 and 3. You will key faster if you think of the numbers in groups.

1 14 134 1431 2343 343123 43 334 3 3421 23214 432442
2 al4 a4231 24 4a24 1432a 34 a4321 a4323 a431 a342 a
3 4343213413 34343213311 4323412341 3431233 44342 43

General Guidelines for Compound Words and Numbers

A hyphen is used to separate some compound words. It is also used in spelled-out numbers.

1. A hyphen is used as a "combining" mark. Not all authorities agree on which combinations should or should not be hyphenated. If in doubt, consult a reference book or dictionary.
   a. As a general rule, use a hyphen between two or more word combinations used as a unit **before** a noun.
      a 15-story building
      the still-active volcano
      a hard-working person
   b. If the word combinations used as a unit appear **after** a noun, do not hyphenate.
      a building 15 stories high
      the volcano that is still active
      a person who is hard working
   c. Words beginning with **ex, self,** and **vice** are usually hyphenated.
      ex-roommate
      self-taught
      vice-principal
2. Hyphenate **spelled-out** fractions and hyphenate **spelled-out** numbers between 21 and 99 if they stand alone or if they are used with numbers over 100. Never hyphenate numerals such as 21 or 66.
   one and one-third
   sixty-six
   one hundred sixty-six

18.7 **THINKING DRILL**

In the Thinking Drill that appears on your screen, you are to apply the guidelines for hyphenating compound words. Follow the instructions on the screen. After you have completed the drill, return to the text and review the information that follows on using dashes.

General Guidelines for the Dash

The dash is often used (1) in place of quotation marks or parentheses, (2) to avoid the confusion of too many commas, (3) for special emphasis, and (4) to indicate a side comment. Study the following examples:

There is a flaw in the plan—a fatal one. [special emphasis]

All books—fiction, poetry, and drama—are on sale. [in place of parentheses]

I cooked the meal—but they got the credit for it. [special emphasis]

I said once—and I will say it again—I disagree. [side comment]

18.8 **THINKING DRILL**

Now you have the opportunity to practice using the dash in a special Thinking Drill that displays on your screen. Follow the directions on the screen. After you complete the drill, you will return to the text for additional key review.

5 Key Drill

Key lines 1–3 twice: first for speed, then for control just as you did for the 4 Key Drill. Anchor the "a" or "f" finger on the home row depending on whether you are keying the numbers 3, 4, 5, or 1, 2, and read the numbers in groups.

1 11 55 a55 11 55 a55 11 55 55 11 51 a51 15 15 15 5
2 55 44 a45 54 14 15 24 25 34 35 53 43 52 42 51 41a
3 15115 15115 a55151 a55151 15 5151 151 al55 a51151

6 Key Drill

Key lines 1–3 twice: first for speed, then for control, just as you did in the 5 Key Drill. Anchor the ";" finger on the home row when keying the number 6.

1 11 a66 11 66 11 66 11 66 11 66 a66 11 66 11 66 61
2 166 166 a661 661 161 161 a611 661 661 116 11 a666
3 11666 16661 61 66 66 111 666 661 1166 16661 61 61

Students in Online Classes

Do not touch the key between the home row and the number key you are entering. This would slow you down; in addition, all keyboards do not have the same alignment.

Additional Drill

Key the following drill. Press ***Enter*** after each line. Concentrate on reading the number in 2-3 combinations.

1 44 44 444 44 44 44 4 4444 44 4 4 444 444 44 44 4 4
2 334 44 343 22343 3443 23423 3422 4321 343 344 43 4
3 43 44342 3431233 4323412341 34343213311 4343213413

4 151 51 55 51 55 15 51 15 15 15 5 5 5 55 55 55 5 5
5 51 15115 155 151 51511 15 55151 55151 15115 15115
6 123 a15a a15a a321 a321a21515 a21515 15115 15115

7 6 61 61 61 61 61 666 666 6 6 6 6 66 66 66 66 6 6 6
8 a666 111 116 661 661 a611 161 161 661 a661 166 166
9 61 61 16661 1166 661 666 111 66 66 61 16661 11666

Sentences

(Omit if Sessions 1–13 have not been completed.)

Key lines 1–10 twice: first for speed, then for control. Follow the same procedure used in the 6 Key Drill above.

1 Dennis and Gene nailed 16 boards onto the old gate.
2 Helen had seen the 12 lighted signs shining at night.
3 Anne and Bill ate a salad and 15 figs and a big steak.

4	Between two consonants **unless**	napkin	*may be divided*	nap-kin
	a root word would be destroyed	billing	*may be divided*	bill-ing (not bil-ling)
5	Between two vowels that are pronounced separately	continuation	*may be divided*	continu-ation
6	**After** a one-syllable vowel rather than **before** (preferable)	benefactor	*may be divided*	bene-factor
	unless the vowel is a part of a suffix	acceptable	*may be divided*	accept-able
7	Between two parts of a compound word	salesperson	*may be divided*	sales-person

8 Do not key more than two consecutive lines ending with hyphens. ***Note:*** Some software packages allow three lines with automatic hyphenation.

Do not divide

9	Words of one syllable	which storm	*never* *never*	wh-ich sto-rm
10	Words with a one-letter prefix	along enough	*not* *not*	a-long e-nough
11	A syllable with a silent vowel sound	yelled strained	*never* *never*	yel-led strain-ed
12	Proper nouns, abbreviations, contractions, or number combinations	Barbara FBI couldn't 31 Oak Lane March 14	*not* *not* *not* *not* *not*	Bar-bara F-BI could-n't 3-1 Oak Lane March 1-4

18.6 Thinking Drill

Now you will have an opportunity to apply the word-division guidelines in a Thinking Drill. Follow the instructions on the screen. After you have completed the drill, return to the text and review the information that follows on using hyphens in compound words and numbers.

4 Leslie sang a tiny jingle as she dashed ahead in glee.
5 When Tom tested his stiff ankle, he gnashed his teeth.
6 Please appease that helpless, pleading, pious plaintiff.

7 A tall, split, peeling aspen sapling is plainly diseased.
8 Pat speaks and pleads and defends the three plaintiffs.
9 Did Tim tape that splint and dispense the correct pills?
10 The spaniel has 134 bites and needs some skilled help.

15.8 NUMBER TIMINGS

Goal: 25 WAM with no more than 2 errors

Take a 1-minute timing on each group of numbers.

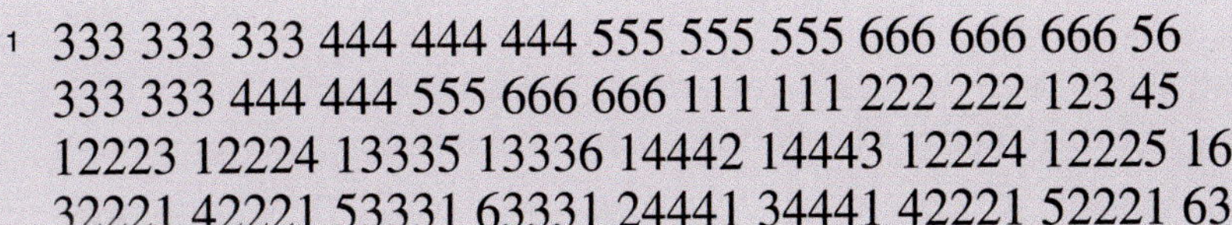

1 333 333 333 444 444 444 555 555 555 666 666 666 56
333 333 444 444 555 666 666 111 111 222 222 123 45
12223 12224 13335 13336 14442 14443 12224 12225 16
32221 42221 53331 63331 24441 34441 42221 52221 63

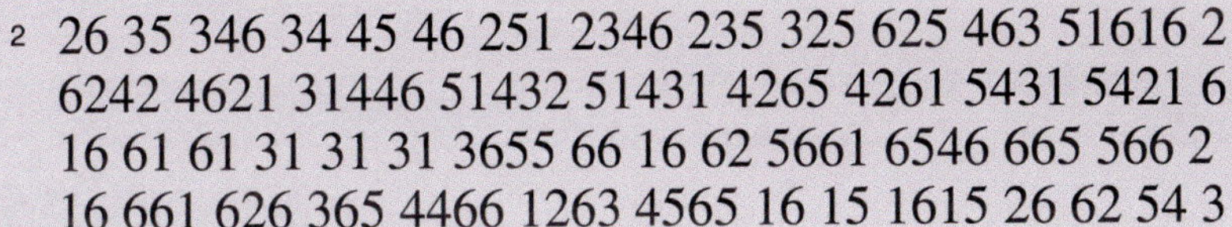

2 26 35 346 34 45 46 251 2346 235 325 625 463 51616 2
6242 4621 31446 51432 51431 4265 4261 5431 5421 6
16 61 61 31 31 31 3655 66 16 62 5661 6546 665 566 2
16 661 626 365 4466 1263 4565 16 15 1615 26 62 54 3

15.9 LETTER TIMINGS

Goal: 30 WAM with no more than 2 errors

Take a 1-minute timing on each paragraph.

3 Over 25 million pagers have been sold. More than half of all pagers sold are for personal use. Parents have beepers so babysitters can reach them when they go out. Adults give their elderly parents and teenagers their beeper number so they can be reached easily. Construction and factory workers use pagers because they do not have easy access to a telephone.

4 Muffin is a genuine bulldog. Although he weighs 64 pounds, he bounds about with a flourish. It is fun to see him plunge around, indulging in the pure pleasure of running. He huffs and puffs and slumps to the ground. No doubt, he will jump and lunge again after a pause and find trouble.

Session 18

HYPHEN, DASH, UNDERSCORE

Session Goals

Hyphen, Dash, Underscore

Hyphenating words
Using dashes

1-Minute: 30 WAM/2 errors
3-Minute: 25 WAM/2 errors

18.1-18.4 On-Screen Exercises: Getting Started

If you are continuing immediately from Session 17, you are already warmed up so start with Exercise 18.2. Click the Next Exercise or Previous Exercise button if you are not at the correct exercise.

If you exited the program at the end of the previous session, refer to page 11, Session 3 for instructions on entering the program.

18.5 On-Screen Exercises: Thinking Drills

This section includes three Thinking Drills that provide practice using the hyphen, dash, and underscore/underline punctuation marks. Then you are to apply the punctuation guidelines in response to questions posed in the Thinking Drills. Read the guidelines for each topic before you key the corresponding drills.

General Guidelines for Word Division

A hyphen is a mark of punctuation used to divide words that must be carried over to the next line. Although most word processing programs offer an automatic hyphenation feature, the software sometimes asks the user to make hyphenation decisions during the hyphenating process. The guidelines that follow include the essential rules. However, there are exceptions to the rules. When in doubt, consult a dictionary.

1 The general rule is to leave at least three letters of a word at the end of a line and carry over at least three letters to the next line. The rule has been modified since software packages leave or carry over only two letters of a word when automatic hyphenation is used.

2 Never divide a word that is the last word of a paragraph or a page.
Divide

3 Between syllables according to pronunciation	provoke	*may be divided*	pro-voke

5 Thomas bought a used car from a dealer at 16532 Halsted Street. Although the bumper and the trunk were ruined, he assumed that it would run. If he would flush the rust from the lumbering hulk of junk, he might be able to use it. His woeful anguish spurred a new thought; perhaps it was useless.

Ending the Session

Now you may print this session's files, continue to the next session, or exit the program. See page 55 of Session 14 if you need to review procedures.

Ergonomic Tip

Keep both feet flat on the floor or a footrest to minimize fatigue.

Unit 3

PUNCTUATION/ SYMBOL KEYS

Session 16

7, 8, 9, 0, COMMA, DECIMAL

Session Goals

7, 8, 9, 0, Comma, Decimal

Numbers (1-Minute): 25 WAM/2 errors
Letters (1-Minute): 30 WAM/2 errors

16.1-16.8 On-Screen Exercises: Getting Started

If you exited the program at the end of the previous session, refer to page 56 of Session 15 to review how to open the next session or to continue from where you left off.

16.9 Textbook Exercises: Reinforcement

Earlier in the session you completed new-key drills presented on the screen. Now you will repeat some of those drills, along with some new drills, to reinforce your keyboarding skills. When you have finished the drills, click Print (if desired), then Next Exercise.

Reviewing the 7, 8, 9, and 0 Keys

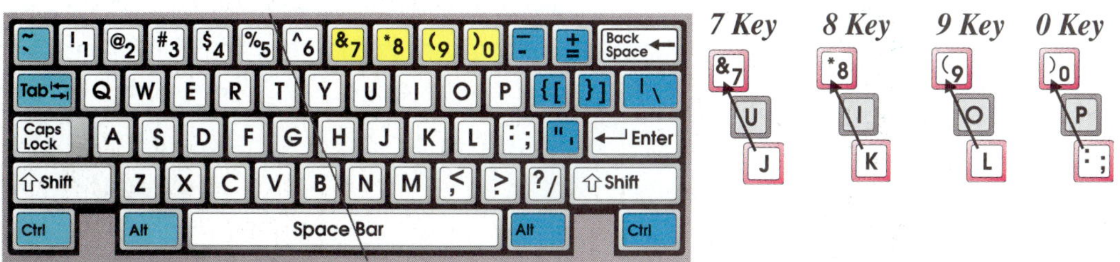

7 Key Drill

Key lines 1–3 twice: first for control, then for speed. Anchor the ";" finger on the home row.

1 a55 77 66 76 57 57 a76 77 777 677 a555 76 6 a755a a755a
2 767 767 5767 5757 a576 7675a 7675a 77 777 666 555 a75a
3 a576a 76a5a 6675a 6675 5667 777 a65a7 5672 a7765 a575a

1 The United States Agency for International Development sponsors a speakers program that provides citizens with an opportunity to learn about the culture of other countries. Educators, business men and women, and school administrators with a need to have firsthand information are eligible. More than 125 countries participate in this program.

2 A career in science involves selecting a path among several options. One could choose to become a doctor in a clinic or a teacher in a medical school. An active search through more than 190 college catalogs will indicate which courses to select. Contact campus finance officers to check cost factors.

3 Mack, a black Scottie, is a champion canine. A constant companion is the yellow cat called Chicco. Crowds laugh and applaud as Mack and Chicco do their tricks to music. Mack can count 15 objects and walk on his hind legs. Chicco jumps over Mack, adding a certain clownish touch to the act.

Ending the Session

Now you may print this session's files, continue to the next session, or exit the program. See page 55 of Session 14 if you need to review procedures.

Ergonomic Tip

You shouldn't have to reach for your keyboard. Move the keyboard so that you can keep your elbows at your side as you position your fingers over the home row keys.

After keying the numbers 7 down to 1, proofread. If you have any errors, repeat the drill until you can key the numbers without error.

See how quickly you can complete the following:

1. Key the numbers 1 through 7 three times. Space once after each number. Keep your eyes on the screen.
2. Reverse the order; key from 7 down to 1. Space once after each number.

8 Key Drill

Key lines 1–3 twice: first for control, then for speed. Anchor either the "j" or the ";" finger on the home row.

1 88 11 588 11 88 11 88 11 88 11 688 11 88 11 8 8823 1482
2 8182 81828 2845 6817 71882 6818 2238 885 888 288 388
3 557 8283 38482 78681 11812 8823 28 28 888 321 854 488

Now complete the following drill to develop speed and concentration:

1. Key the numbers 1 through 8 three times. Space once between numbers. Again, keep your eyes on the screen. Do not look at your fingers.
2. Reverse the order; key from 8 back to 1 three times. Space once between numbers.

9 Key Drill

Key lines 1–3 twice for control. Anchor the "j" finger at home as the "l" finger keys 9. Remember to read the numbers as groups.

1 8489 19891 1919 1891 9981 19867 183218 189 19 698 98
2 99 88 589 998 998 888 991 999 498 98 99 88 94 32989 29
3 23 1989 2239 39823 59891 123 698 92919 9812 375 688 9

Here's another drill to develop speed with the 9 key:

1. Key the numbers 1 through 9 three times. Space once between numbers. Remember keep your eyes on the screen.
2. Reverse the order; key from 9 back to 1 three times. Again, space once between numbers.

0 (Zero) Key Drill

Key the following line three times for control. Anchor the "j" finger at home as the ";" finger strikes 0.

Note: Be sure to use the zero key, not the capital O.

10 20 30 40 50 60 70 80 90 a10 a20 a30 240 250 10 115 619 057

Now try this drill to help you focus on the location of each number key:

1. Key the numbers from 1 to 100. Space once after each number. Use word wrap.
2. Key the numbers from 2 to 200 by twos. Space once after each number. Again, use word wrap.

If the fraction appears alone or does not express a direct physical measurement, spell out the fraction.

He makes only half of what she makes.

9 Use figures to express decimals.

He is 6.5 feet tall.

10 For ages, follow the general guidelines for numbers.

He is 20 years old.
She is nine months old.

11 Use figures to express clock time.

Pack your bags right away so we can make the 5:20 p.m. flight.

12 Key house numbers in figures.

His address is 13038 N. Westgate Drive.

13 Spell out street names that contain numbers ten or below; if the numbers are above ten, express the names in figures.

The store is located on First Avenue.
My address is 17815 N. 13th Avenue.

Sentences

Key lines 1–10 twice: first for speed, then for control.

1 Did Van ever deliver the varnish and the 150 shelves?
2 Vinnie lives in their villa; he enjoys the vast veranda.
3 It is evident; the vital lever reverses the vexing vent.

4 Ron delivered the 18 leather chairs late this evening.
5 Marvel served 286 vanilla shakes at two gala events.
6 The driver developed a fever; give him 13 vitamins.

7 That starving animal evaded 103 vigilant observers.
8 She does not fool them; she is not an honest senator.
9 Opal ordered the onions and olives from the market.
10 Did the florist remove all the thorns from the roses?

17.5 ONE-MINUTE TIMINGS

Goal: 30 WAM with no more than 2 errors
Take a 1-minute timing on each paragraph.

Number Concentration Drill

Key lines 1–5 twice for control. Concentrate on reading the numbers in groups.

1 11201 1316 14037 22304 3405 4506 35607 6708 78092 1415
2 6816z 62317 73218 2219 32206 8782 19222 90234 1929 3030
3 45317 7932 34332 13476 9535 87369 1370 1743 37744 7645

4 2674 65647 1674 84859 34750 25151 23270 45524 8910 573
5 91524 7853 85426 1927 52938 22304 11201 78092 7753 361

Comma and Decimal Keys

You have now been introduced to all ten digits and are ready to review other areas of the keyboard. There are two symbols used frequently with numbers—the ***comma*** and the ***decimal point*** (also used as a period at the end of a sentence). These keys were reviewed in Session 3 but because they are used frequently with numbers, more practice is offered here.

Comma Key

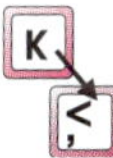

Decimal Key

Comma Key Drill

When numbers are separated by commas, decimals, spaces, letters, or other symbols, use those division points as natural breaks between groups of numbers. For example, 5,134 would be read ***five/comma/one thirty-four.***

Key lines 1–3 twice: first for control, then for speed. Concentrate on grouping the numbers by division points.

1 1,368 16,434 92,860 58,167 34,511 76,924 6,331 21,468
2 38,107 48,243 1,509 5,114 15,816 6,184,336 98,165,225
3 4,408,452 251,145 12,259 1,259 159,467 43,410 875,243

Decimal Key Drill

Key lines 1–3 for control. Concentrate on reading numbers by division points. If you make a mistake, start over until you complete the line without an error.

1 41,345.51 15,378.78 31,428.27 89,261,500.68 59.63 61.3
2 91,007.23 851,267.18 109.01 13.17 8.43 4.40 596.27 39.8
3 990.85 67,349.34 23,265.08 186.84 4.23 .87 8,582 13.455

7 4559 71.26 8674005 21 4.86 489,753 4605141 50 224
8 531 78911 556 9,454.89 49724301 5,410 8.26 667101
9 2,466 61780 434215 5436 33216 4457004 96.48 82 46

Important: If you have not completed Sessions 1–13 (the alphabetic keys), go to Ending the Session. Otherwise proceed to the General Guidelines for Expressing Numbers and read and key each of the examples.

General Guidelines for Expressing Numbers

Authorities do not always agree on when to spell out numbers and when to use figures. The guidelines illustrated here are those that are widely accepted.

Key the examples for each guideline. Read what you have keyed so that you have a mental image of the applications for the guidelines.

1 Spell out numbers one through ten; use figures for numbers 11 and above.

The computer science class includes six women.
At least 40 men are enrolled in beginning keyboarding.

2 If any of the numbers in a series is above ten, use figures for all the numbers.

We have 16 Compaq computers, 14 Dell computers, and 8 Gateway computers.

3 When a sentence begins with a number, spell it out (or rewrite the sentence).

Three hundred students are majoring in business.
Business majors number 300.

4 If the day of the month precedes the month, express it in words.

We will meet on the sixth of December.

5 If the day of the month follows the month, express it in figures.

We will meet on December 6 at the restaurant.

6 If the date is in the form of month, day, and year, express the day and year in figures. ***Note:*** Always follow the year with a comma unless it appears at the end of a sentence.

We will meet on December 6, 2007, at the restaurant.

7 Use figures for measurements, percentages, and other mathematical expressions.

We need new carpet for a room that is 11 feet x 12 feet.
The package weighs about 7 pounds.
I will ask for a 6 percent raise.

8 Generally, use figures to express fractions and mixed numbers in technical writing or in physical measurements.

They used 3.5 feet of coaxial cable.

Additional Drill

Key the following drill for speed. Press ***Enter*** after each line.

1 77 77 7 7777 7777 777 777 77 77 7 7 7777 777 77 7
2 6 76 a555 677 777 77 a76 57 57 76 66 77 a55 75 75
3 4651 1234 3467 461234 3457 56712 62345 5671 71234

4 88 88 88 88 88 888 888 88 88 8 8 8 88 88 88 8 8 8
5 8 11 88 11 688 11 88 11 88 11 88 11 588 11 88 411
6 88 2238 6818 71882 6817 2845 81828 8182 1482 8823

7 91 999 99 9 999 9 99 99 99 91 91 91 99 9 999 9 99
8 19 189 183218 19867 9981 1891 1919 19891 8489 989
9 92919 698 123 59891 39823 2239 1989 2923 32989 94

10 10 20 30 40 50 60 70 80 90 a10 a20 a30 240 250 10
11 6,151 6,719 1,438 4,497 5,313 7,893 38,751 45,134
12 .87 4.23 186.84 23,265.08 67,349.34 990.85 596.27

Sentences

(Omit if Sessions 1–13 have not been completed.)

Key lines 1–10 twice: first for speed, then for control.

1 Of the 15,220 rangers, 170 sprained their ankles last year.
2 Dirk did the drills first and drank the delicious tea later.
3 Take 12 or 13 fresh, green grapes as your dessert treat.

4 He risks great danger if he departs after the dinner.
5 The 14 interns gratefully lingered in the green garden.
6 The meat manager made a simple remark and smirked.

7 Did Mary send the 380 messages after amending them?
8 Pam had made some malts with milk, mint, and mango.
9 The firefighters attempted an immense task and missed.
10 Did Sammie eliminate the 16 mistakes in the message?

16.10 NUMBER TIMINGS

Goal: 25 WAM with no more than 2 errors

- Take a 1-minute timing on each group of numbers.
- Press ***Enter*** at the end of each line.

Key lines 1–3 twice: first for control, then for speed. Concentrate on reading numbers in groups.

1 1,676,352.17 3,131 2.24 436,342 101.31 166,891 89
2 236,731 831,643 534.67 4,091,867 3,587.13 501,316
3 61,301.04 .36 89,341.76 31,700.73 151,317 416,319

Creating Columns of Numbers

Using the preset tabs every 0.5 inches, create the columns of numbers shown below by keying the first four-digit number and then pressing ***Tab*** twice to move between columns. Press ***Enter*** at end of the line.

4901	8702	3303	3904	7205
6106	8307	9408	2709	3710
1511	5712	2613	9114	1515
5716	9117	5618	6619	3820
2621	3122	4523	2324	3125
6726	3528	8528	3529	4130
7731	6932	8533	7434	9935
8836	2337	6138	1639	5840

Students in Online Classes

It is faster to keep groups of numbers in columns by moving across the columns using the tab feature. Keying all the numbers in a column and then moving to the next column is slower.

Numbers Drill

Key lines 1–3 twice: first for control, then for speed. Remember to read the numbers in 2-3-2 combinations.

1 7371130 91368840 1534986003 51673455189 963310931
2 21468159 515113 6873931 438761 223026501 89340013
3 6135910 619822385 3676 1090101 3948131 1788434341

Additional Drill

Key the following drill for control. Press ***Enter*** after each line.

1 2 34141 38886190 1 5133459 789 386005138 45134157
2 9,586,713 39,913,867 55,565,577 231,464 2,361,731
3 4,131 59.39 13,667 63,485 .98 78,431 40.83 76,924

4 47 681107 741 23 15281 59,602,388 2.95 96175 284 4
5 56451089 904 82 67,832,523.15 571.28 903 84.22 99
6 15 510 67414451 281,401,282.00 61700 29.15 106 80

1 .81 85 823 8466 8877 7868 58 45 238 845 866 8143 8 8123 5671 82345 3458 8612348 3467 1238 886 81387 5834278 58743218 11386518 2251386 87 88 8811318 8 5481 8375 18 2368 8 7628 81 61842 8811318 18 8788 5792 6139 144

2 91 95 923 8466 9977 7898 69 45 239 945 966 9143 9 9123 5671 92345 3458 9612349 3467 12392 996 81389 5934278 59743219 11386519 2251396 973 99 9911319 9 5491 9375 19 2368 9 7629 947 61942 99111319 19 979 7426 5187 239

3 27 821 59361 40352 89734 92035 64019 9356 693 958 3177 501 6512 96 8742 56034 56832 85923 780 847 91 6409 7483 9467 3520 5945 2635 5705 8932 6485 1956 23670 81251800 165 208125635 69312 9871 6017340 2 716941 8320193 5163 8613 5113818 8542001 88490 6 2361 15432 11621618 11234 19051 3399 668 45441 4091 25937 68465 21893 492 591 783

16.11 LETTER TIMINGS

Goal: 30 WAM with no more than 2 errors

Take a 1-minute timing on each paragraph.

1 Zeb went to the zoo to see the 179 new animals. He went especially to see the 18 species of lizards. He wants to be a zoologist when he gets older. He knows many things about animals, and his parents are really amazed.

2 A cookout on the beach could include 6 kinds of cheese, carrots, 3 types of meat sandwiches, and 14 cans of cold juice. If the chill of the ocean is too much, hot chocolate and hot coffee can chase the cold chills. The decent lunch and a chat with friends can enrich affection.

3 An office clerk who lacks basic ethics could become the subject of scorn. Those who gossip about or verbally abuse new workers can cause problems. It is smart to follow the 13 rules that are printed on the bulletin board about getting along with fellow workers. Do the right thing and be sincere.

ENDING THE SESSION

Now you may print this session's files, continue to the next session, or exit the program. See page 55 of Session 14 if you need to review procedures.

Ergonomic Tip

The human body is made to move. When you stay in one position too long, you will end up stiff, sore, and stressed. After sitting at your workstation for 45-60 minutes, stand up and stretch your arms and legs.

NUMBER PATTERNS USING PRESET TABS

Session Goals

Number patterns
Use preset tabs

Letters (1-Minute): 30 WAM/2 errors

Use preset tabs

17.1-17.3 On-Screen Exercises: Getting Started

If you exited the program at the end of the previous session, refer to page 56 of Session 15 to review how to open the next session or to continue from where you left off.

17.4 Textbook Exercises: Reinforcement

Some of the drills that were presented on-screen during the first part of Session 17 are repeated here, along with some new drills, to reinforce your keyboarding skills. When you have finished the drills, click Print (if desired), then Next Exercise.

Keying Numbers

Complete these drills to reinforce your number keying skills:

1 Key this line of numbers two times:

11 22 33 44 55 66 77 88 99 00

2 The most frequently used number is 0, followed by 5. To build your skills with these numbers, first key to 500 by tens; then key to 200 by fives.

Example: 10 20 30 40 50 60 etc.
Example: 5 10 15 20 25 30 35 40 45 50 etc.

3 To reinforce your ability to think while keying numbers, start at 100 and key to 0 by threes.

Example: 100 97 94 91 88 85 82 79 etc.

Repeat these drills whenever you can. They will help you master numbers.

Reading Number Groups

Remember, when numbers are grouped naturally by commas, spaces, and decimals, read the number by those groups. For example, 1,676,352.17 is read ***one/comma/six seventy-six/comma/three fifty-two/decimal/seventeen.***

Creating Documents

One of the options available with the Paradigm Keyboarding software is the Paradigm Word Processor (PWP). You can access PWP by clicking Word Processor on the Snap menu bar, and then clicking the hyperlink to launch PWP. This takes you into a new document window of the word processing program where you can create various types of documents including memorandums (memos), e-mail messages, personal business letters, and manuscripts. Many other kinds of documents can also be created in PWP since it is a working word processor.

When creating documents of any kind, there are certain rules of formatting to follow. Formatting varies depending on the type of document you are creating. To help you create some of the most common documents used today, the following examples explain the purpose of each document and its proper formatting.

Remember, you are ready to create a new document once you are in the Word Processor. You can find guidelines for saving, naming, printing, closing, and opening a document in the PWP Quick Reference Guide, which follows this appendix. Feel free to tear this guide out of the book and use it as a desktop reference.

Preparing a Memorandum (Memo) or an E-Mail

Preparing a widely used document, such as a memo or an e-mail, provides you with an opportunity to integrate and apply the keyboarding skills that you have been developing. Memorandums (memos for short) and e-mail are the most frequently used documents in business globally. Memos and e-mail are very similar and consist of a four-part heading plus the body (message) as shown in the example that follows:

DATE: (current date)
(ds)
TO: (name of the person to receive the memo or the person's E-mail address)
(ds)
FROM: (your name)
(ds)
SUBJECT: (THE SUBJECT OF YOUR MEMO OR E-MAIL IN ALL CAPS)

(press enter 3 times)

The body includes the information you want to communicate to the receiver. Note that the body is single-spaced with a double space between paragraphs. Indenting the first line of each paragraph is not necessary. The blank space between paragraphs is adequate to show where one paragraph ends and another begins.

(ds)

The memo starts one inch from the top of the page, which is the default. Use the default left and right margins of PWP. You can begin entering the date line on the first line on your screen. Note: The introductory headings of the memo (DATE, TO, FROM, SUBJECT) can appear in a different order, depending on the memo style.

(ds)

E-mail formatting will automatically insert the current date and your name. An example of an E-mail name (address) would be tmodl@emcp.com. An additional E-mail heading may include COURTESY COPY (Cc:). This optional heading allows you to send a copy to another individual by filling in the proper E-mail address.

(ds)

your initials/filename

Preparing a Personal Business Letter

The business letter is another important communication tool. Although a memo is used to convey information internally, a letter is used to transmit information to or from individuals outside a company or organization. Just as memos have their distinct parts, so do letters. Study the example that follows:

(2 inches from top of page)

Current date

(press enter 4-7 times)

Mr. Matt Loid, President
Loid Printing Services
4962 St. Andrews Circle
Portland, OR 80333-4452

(ds)

Dear Mr. Loid:

(ds)

Our communications class is planning a series of intense studies on various aspects of desktop publishing. As part of this series, we would like to visit a printing firm that is known for modern and innovative practices.

(ds)

Our class meets Monday through Friday from 8:30 a.m. to 11:30 a.m. Would it be possible for our class to visit your firm sometime during the month of February? If so, please contact me at 555-9462 any day after 3:30 p.m.

continued

(ds)
Sincerely yours,

(press enter 4 times)

Rosemarie Jenkins
425 Second Street
Portland, OR 80378-5103

Most business letters are printed on letterhead paper that provides information about the organization (name, address, city, state, ZIP, e-mail address, phone number). Letters from an individual not representing an organization are generally prepared on plain paper. These letters are called personal business letters.

The personal business letter begins with the date line followed by four to seven lines and then the inside address. The inside address contains the name of the person receiving the letter, his/her organization, and address. The inside address is followed by a double space and then a greeting or salutation. In the block-style letter, all of these lines begin at the left margin.

The body of the letter is single-spaced with a double space between paragraphs. At the end of the document, there is a double space followed by the complimentary closing. Allow four lines after the closing to leave sufficient room for the writer's signature. The signature block, which contains the writer's name and address, is keyed under the closing.

Preparing a Manuscript

A manuscript is a document containing one or several pages and is used for research reports, magazine or journal articles, or term papers for a particular course. Short manuscripts consisting of one to four pages are usually formatted as an unbound manuscript. A manuscript may contain multiple headings that need proper formatting. The rules for headings, page numbering, and line spacing are as follows:

- **Major title:** Key on approximately line 6 of the first page; center and bold the title; capitalize all letters; double-space to the first-level heading (if used) or to the first line of the body.
- **First-level heading:** Center, bold and capitalize the first letter of each major word; double-space above and below.
- **Second-level heading:** Place it flush with the left margin on a separate line; capitalize the first letter of each major word; bold the heading; double-space above and below.
- **Third-level heading:** Indent with paragraph; capitalize only first letter or first word followed by a colon or period; underscore; double-space before. Note that some manuscript sections have second-level headings only, while others may have second-level headings followed by third-level headings.
- **Page Numbering:** Place page numbers in the upper-right corner beginning with page 2 and leave a double space between the number and the body.
- **Spacing:** Use double spacing throughout.

PROPER TELEPHONE TECHNIQUES

(ds)

The Business Image

(ds)

It is widely accepted that proper use of the telephone as a business tool is one important quality of an outstanding employee. Most office workers spend two or more hours each day in telephone contact with

clients and customers.

(ds)

Caller's Response

(ds)

A prompt answer. Answering the telephone promptly will give the caller a favorable impression of the company. Use a lively, pleasant

voice that creates a welcoming atmosphere.

PWP QUICK REFERENCE

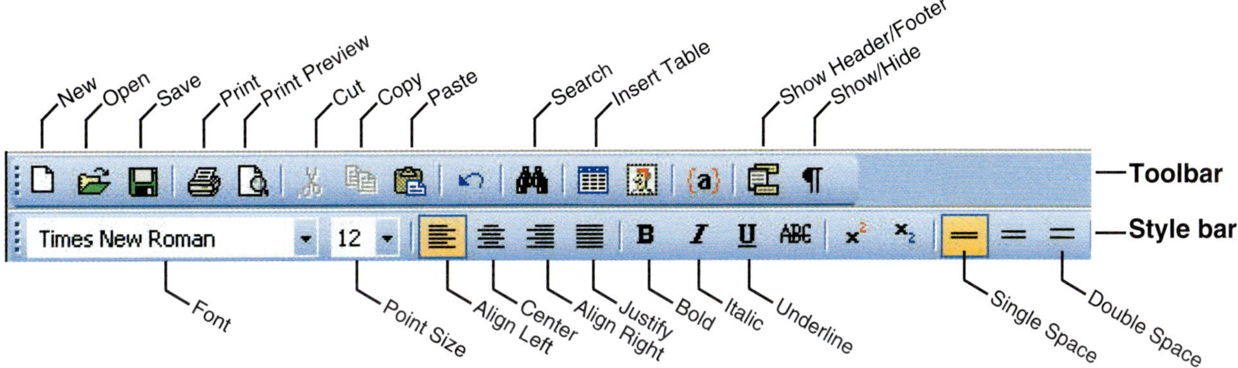

Opening a PWP Document

Many times you will want to open a document that has been saved. You may want to bring it back to the screen to add more text, review the document, or make corrections. To open a saved document, complete the following steps:

1. At the PWP window, click the Open button on the toolbar or choose File→Open. ***Note:*** You can select a pull-down menu such as File from the top of the screen by either clicking it with the mouse or by pressing the ***Alt*** key and the underlined letter key at the same time.
2. At the *Open* dialog box a list of documents is displayed. Note: If you cannot locate your document, check the Look in box located toward the top of the dialog box, and make sure the drive listed in the box is the same drive where you saved your documents. The *Open* dialog box lists all documents saved in folder in alphabetic (or numeric) order.
3. Position the mouse pointer on the document name and click the left button to select the document.
4. Press Enter or click Open to open the document. ***Note:*** You can also double-click (two clicks in quick succession) with the left mouse button on the document name to open the document.

Saving a PWP Document

You can save a newly created document in PWP by taking the following steps:

1. Choose File→Save As.
2. At the *Save As* dialog box, key in the document name in the File name text box, then click Save or press ***Enter***.

You can save an opened document in PWP by doing *one* of the following steps:

1. Choose File→Save.
2. Clicking the Save button on the toolbar.
3. Pressing ***Ctrl + S.***

Naming a PWP Document

A document name in Windows can be from 1 to 255 characters in length. It can contain letters (uppercase or lowercase), numbers, spaces, periods, and some symbols. PKB automatically adds a period and three-character extension to a file name. You will receive specific instructions for naming files in the text.

Printing a PWP Document

1. Open the document you wish to print.
2. Click the Print button on the toolbar or choose File→Print.
3. Click OK in the *Print* dialog box.

Closing a PWP Document

To close a document in PWP,

1. Save the document.
2. Choose File→Close.

Deleting a PWP Document

To delete a document in PWP,

1. Click the Open button on the toolbar or choose File→Open.
2. At the Open dialog box, position the arrow pointer on the name of the document you wish to delete, and then click the right mouse button.
3. At the pop-up menu that displays, click Delete with the left mouse button.
4. At the question asking if you are sure you want to delete the document, click Yes.
5. Click the Cancel button to close the Open dialog box.

Note: In PWP, you cannot delete a document that is currently opened.